VICTORY
OVER THE DARKNESS

STUDY GUIDE

NEIL T. ANDERSON

Gospel Light

PUBLISHING STAFF
William T. Greig, Publisher
Dr. Elmer L. Towns, Senior Consulting Publisher
Dr. Gary S. Greig, Senior Consulting Editor
Pam Weston, Editor
Patti Pennington Virtue, Assistant Editor
Christi Goeser, Editorial Assistant
Kyle Duncan, Associate Publisher
Bayard Taylor, M.Div., Senior Editor, Theological and Biblical Issues
Kevin Parks, Cover Designer
Debi Thayer, Designer
Lisa Guest, Contributing Writer

Rights for publishing this book in other languages are contracted by Gospel Light Worldwide, the international nonprofit ministry of Gospel Light. Gospel Light Worldwide also provides publishing and technical assistance to international publishers dedicated to producing Sunday School and Vacation Bible School curricula and books in the languages of the world. For additional information, visit www.gospellightworldwide.org; write to Gospel Light Worldwide, P.O. Box 3875, Ventura, CA 93006; or send an e-mail to info@gospellightworldwide.org.

Contents

A Note from Neil Anderson

Luke 5:1-11 is my favorite account of how the Lord taught. Jesus was instructing the multitudes from Peter's boat. "And when He had finished speaking, He said to Simon, 'Put out into the deep water and let down your nets for a catch'" (v. 4). Jesus had stopped talking, but He had not stopped teaching. Peter heard what Jesus said, but he hadn't learned until he got into the boat and put out the nets.

This study guide gives you an opportunity to get into the boat and put out the nets. You can do it alone, but I recommend that you do it with other faithful learners. It provides an opportunity for more collective wisdom, and greater learning always takes place in the context of committed relationships. Developing trusting relationships and being devoted to one another in prayer are what make group study so enriching.

I am thankful for the tremendous work that Lisa Guest did in putting together the first edition of this study guide. Another helpful resource is *Breaking Through to Spiritual Maturity* (Gospel Light, 1992, revised 2000), a curriculum for teaching these truths in a Sunday School class or small group. Since all this material has been professionally videotaped, you may want to consider an hour of video instruction each week and then use this study guide for group interaction. A summary of resources available from Freedom in Christ Ministries is given at the end of this study guide.

It is my prayer that you will fully realize who you are in Christ and learn to live as a child of God. If this study guide helps make that possible, I will be thankful. May the grace and love of our heavenly Father bless you with all the riches of your inheritance in Christ.

Neil T. Anderson

Chapter 1

Who Are You?

Jesus promises His people that "You shall know the truth, and the truth shall make you free" (John 8:32). Our identity in Jesus Christ is a fundamental truth that we believers need to understand if we are to experience this promised freedom and to grow to Christian maturity.

Who Are You?

(pages 23-24)

"Who are you?" It sounds like a simple question, but attempting to answer it soon reveals the complexity of the issue. How would you answer the question if someone asked you, "Who are you?"

We tend to identify ourselves and each other by what we look like, what we do, and perhaps even by our theological position, our denominational preference or our role in the church. But is who you are determined by what you do, look like and believe in? Or is what you do, look like and believe in determined by who you are? That's an important question, especially as it relates to Christian maturity.

- Neil Anderson believes that your hope for growth, meaning and fulfillment as a Christian is based on understanding who you are, specifically, your identity in Christ as a child of God. Your understanding of who God is and who you are in relationship to Him is the critical foundation for your belief system and your behavior patterns as a Christian.

Do you naturally identify yourself as a child of God as you think about who you are? Why or why not?

Where in your own life do you see a connection between your belief system and your behavior patterns? Give an example or two of how your beliefs about yourself influence your behavior.

What changes in your behavior might result if you were able to clearly see yourself as the much-loved child of God that you are?

False Equations in the Search for Identity

(pages 24-28)

- Neil tells of an attractive 17-year-old girl who, from the outside, seemed to have everything going for her: excellent grades, musical talent, a full-ride university scholarship, a wonderful wardrobe and a brand new car.

    Upon talking with Mary, Neil quickly realized that what was on the inside didn't match the outside. He asked Mary, "Have you ever cried yourself to sleep at night because you felt inadequate and wished you were somebody else?" Through her tears, she asked, "How did you know?"

What does your appearance suggest about you? What do you think people see as they look at you?

Perhaps, like Mary, you have felt inadequate and wished you were somebody else. How does what is inside you differ from your outward appearance? Comment on any discrepancy between your outward appearance and your inner reality.

Shame, fear, insecurity, loneliness, past hurts—there are many reasons why people, intentionally or otherwise, hide their real selves from others. Why do you hide your real self under an outside appearance that is so different from what is inside?

• Often what we show on the outside is a false front arising from our belief that if we appear attractive, perform well or enjoy a certain amount of status, then we will have it all together inside as well. But such is not the case. You plus attractiveness, you plus good performance and you plus status do not equal wholeness and significance. The only identity equation that works in God's kingdom is you plus Christ. Only you plus Christ equal wholeness and meaning.

How did you learn that being attractive, performing well or earning status does not mean wholeness or does not win you love?

In what area(s) of your life has Christ given you the wholeness and meaning you once were seeking?

In what area(s) of your life would you like Jesus to give you wholeness and meaning?

In God's kingdom, everyone has the same opportunity for a meaningful life. Why? Because wholeness and meaning in life are not products of what you have or don't have, what you've done or haven't done. In Christ you are already a whole person positionally and you already possess a life of infinite meaning and purpose because of who you are—a child of God.

- Although a Christian's identity in Christ is the key to wholeness, many believers have difficulty with their identity, security, significance, spiritual maturity and sense of worth. Ignorance is probably the primary reason (see Hosea 4:6). For others it is carnality, or the lack of repentance and faith in God, and for some it is deception by the father of lies (see John 8:44).

What false ideas might you have about who you are?

Asking a person about false ideas about him- or herself may be like asking fish about the water they swim in. The individual can't see what is so much a part of his or her reality. If you're not sure which ideas about yourself are false, ask someone you trust to help you see yourself as God sees you. Also, spend some time in prayer asking God to help you see yourself through His eyes.

- Neil tells of a young woman convinced that she was evil. While she may have done some evil things, at the core of her being she wasn't evil, as evidenced by the deep remorse she felt after sinning. She did, however, let Satan's accusations about her behavior influence her perception of herself instead of believing the truth.

In what ways are you trapped in this same downward spiral? Have you, for instance, failed at something and therefore see yourself as a failure? Are you basing your identity on something you've done rather than on who you are as a child of God? Be specific, and then, as you pray about this downward spiral, thank God that He sees you as His child.

Why would it be to your disadvantage to focus on the missteps you've taken in your life?

When we swallow Satan's lie and believe that what we do determines who we are, that false belief sends us into a tailspin of hopelessness and more defeat.

The Original Creation

(pages 28-32)

Genesis 1 and 2 tell how God created Adam and Eve in His image which gives us the capacity to fully think, feel and choose. After God breathed life into his nostrils, Adam was both physically and spiritually alive (see Genesis 1:26,27). For the Christian, to be spiritually alive is to be in union with God by being in Christ. And that union with God means three important things for believers.

Significance—In the original creation, humankind was given a divine purpose—dominion over all the other creatures. As a restored child of God, you have important work to do for your Lord.

Safety and Security—In the garden of Eden, Adam and Eve's needs were cared for. Likewise, we who follow Christ lack nothing. Safety and security is another facet of our inheritance in Christ.

Belonging—A true sense of belonging comes not only from knowing that we belong to God but also from belonging to each other just as God created Eve to provide a meaningful, open, sharing relationship for Adam.

Which of these is most appealing to you right now? Why?

Which of these seems most unreachable to you? Why?

Significance, safety and security, and belonging were no longer human attributes once sin entered the world.

The Effects of the Fall

(pages 32-38)

The effects of man's fall were dramatic, immediate and far-reaching, infecting every subsequent member of the human race—infecting you. We'll look at five effects of the Fall.

Spiritual Death

- With the Fall, Adam and Eve's union with God was severed. They were separated from God.

When did you first become aware of your separation from God? What circumstances brought you to the realization that you needed God?

Maybe you're just now realizing your need for God. In a brief prayer, tell Him of your need and how you have fallen short of being the person He wants you to be. Read 1 John 1:9 and thank God for the gift of His forgiveness. Cleansed and forgiven because of Jesus' death on your behalf, accept Jesus as your Savior and ask Him to help you live with Him as Lord of your life. (**Note:** It is important to find a church body that will help you grow in your knowledge of and commitment to God.)

Lost Knowledge of God

- The Fall affected the way Adam and Eve (and you and I) think. The fact that Adam and Eve tried to hide from God (see Genesis 3:7,8) clearly indicates a faulty understanding of who God is.

When have you tried to hide from God? What prompted that attempt?

Are you trying to hide from God right now? If so, what is causing you to do this? Read Psalm 23. Hear God's words of love for you. Believe the truth that you have no reason to hide from a loving and forgiving God.

- In God's original design, knowledge was relational. When Adam and Eve lost their relationship with God, they lost the knowledge of God that was intrinsic to that relationship. In our unregenerate state, we know something about God, but we don't know God because we have a broken relationship with Him. When we enter God's family, however, we can know God as Adam and Eve did.

Describe the differences in your life once you took the step from knowing *about* God to *knowing* Him. How is the after picture different from the before picture? How are you a different person now that you know God personally?

In Christ we are able to know God personally because we have received the mind of Christ in our inner selves at salvation (see 1 Corinthians 2:16).

Dominant Negative Emotions

• Not only did the Fall affect humankind's thinking, it also affected us emotionally.

For one thing, we have become fearful and anxious. What fears dominated your life before you realized that you are a child of God? (The fact that these fears may continue to intrude doesn't make you less of a Christian.)

Another emotional by-product of sin is shame and guilt. What have been some sources of shame and guilt in your life?

Humankind also became depressed and angry after the Fall. What events and circumstances trigger your feelings of depression and/or anger?

Fear and anxiety, shame and guilt, depression and anger: what would God have you do with these powerful and destructive emotions?

In Genesis 4, God talks to an angry Cain about his feelings and says, "If you do what is right, will you not be accepted?" (Genesis 4:7, *NIV*). In other words, if you do what is right, you won't feel angry and depressed. When have you noticed that bad feelings follow wrong behavior and/or good feelings follow right behavior? Be specific.

Think about your life right now. What changes in your actions need to be made in light of the truth about the relationship between feelings and behavior?

Too Many Choices

- The Fall affected our wills to choose as well as our thinking and our emotions. In the garden, everything that Adam and Eve wanted to do was okay except eating from the tree of the knowledge of good and evil (see Genesis 2:16,17). One result of their bad choice to eat from that tree is the myriad of good and bad choices you and I face every day.

Which choices that you face bring into clearest focus the sharp contrast between your will and what God would have you do?

What can you do to insure that your choices are the choices God would have you make?

Attributes Become Needs

- Another long-term effect of sin is that humankind's glowing attributes before the Fall became glaring needs after the Fall. Acceptance was replaced by rejection, so we feel the need to belong.

When you have felt the need to be accepted by God and/or by people, what steps have you taken to meet that need?

How has God met this need in your life? How can you help meet the needs of others?

- Innocence was replaced by guilt and shame, so we need our legitimate sense of worth restored.

If you have a low sense of worth, if you are your own harshest critic or if you have a hard time liking yourself, what have you done (or what could you do) to overcome this?

How is your identity as a child of God—or how might your identity in Christ be—the means to overcome a negative self-image?

- Dominion was replaced by weakness and helplessness, so we strive for strength and self-control.

How have you, during times of weakness and helplessness, found strength and peace in the Lord? Be specific about the circumstances.

Neil Anderson observed that "the human soul was not designed to function as a master. You cannot serve God and wealth" (see Matthew 6:24). Consider how you spend your time, your talents and your money. Who or what are you serving and, if you can figure that out, why?

- We human beings have several basic needs. Since the Fall, we've had the need to belong, the need to have our legitimate sense of worth restored and the need to have strength and self-control.

As Neil Anderson observes, "Every temptation is an attempt by the devil to get us to live our lives independently of God. Satan tempts us as he did Jesus by appealing to our most basic and legitimate needs." What evidence from your own life supports this observation? In other words, when have your attempts to meet basic needs led you to sin? Know that, as one who calls Jesus "Lord," you are forgiven for the sins you confess (see 1 John 1:9).

As God's unique creation, you have significance. As a child of God, you can find safety and security. As a member of God's family, you can experience a sense of belonging.

LIVING WHAT YOU LEARN

Guided by the truths of this chapter, answer the question, "Who are you?" Through the week, use some of the answers to who you are to counter any negative thoughts you have about yourself.

A WORD OF PRAYER

Father God,

It is a privilege to be Your child. It is a gift of grace I don't fully comprehend. I thank You for Your wondrous love for me, and I ask that You would help me lead a life that honors You. Help me live according to the truth that my identity is based on who I am in Christ. May I see myself through Your eyes. May I understand more clearly how much You love me and let that love empower and guide me. I pray in the name of Jesus Christ through whom You graciously demonstrated Your amazing love for sinful me. Amen.

LOOKING AHEAD

As a believer, your true identity is not based on what you do or what you possess but on who you are in Christ. You will better understand who you are in Christ when you see how Jesus won back for you the identity that was lost when man was expelled from the garden. Christ's triumph and what it has gained for you are the themes of the next chapter.

The Whole Gospel

As we've seen, many Christians are not living free and productive lives because they don't understand their identities and positions in Christ. Until they see themselves the way God sees them, they can't fully understand the gospel and the dramatic change that occurred the moment they trusted in Christ.

The Whole Gospel

(pages 41-43)

- Remember the story of Bill and the example of Eric Liddle?

  What does the story of Bill say to you about the race you are running for the Lord, your focus and your fitness?

Olympic runner Eric Liddle withdrew from a race scheduled on Sunday—a race he might have won—in honor of his heavenly Father. When has your commitment to the Lord caused you to take a stand that many people around you didn't understand?

We Christians are salt and light in a dying and dark world because of the dramatic change that occurs in us the moment we trust in Jesus.

The Example of Christ

Too many Christians identify with the first Adam—with the Adam who sinned and was exiled from the presence of God. In reality, however, Christians are identified with Jesus Christ, the last Adam. As a result, the difference in your history is eternally profound. You need to be sure you're identifying with the right Adam, with Jesus your Savior.

- What we notice about Jesus is His complete dependence on God the Father.

Where do you struggle and, like the first Adam, even fail to depend completely on God? What areas of your life (attitudes, responsibilities, etc.) are you reluctant to surrender to God?

What keeps you from trusting God and depending on Him completely? Confess those barriers that keep you from trusting and ask God to help your lack of faith (see Mark 9:24).

When have you taken a step of faith and found God faithful beyond your greatest expectations? Describe that experience in detail and let it serve as a touchstone the next time you need to step out in faith.

Where do you have the opportunity to take a step of faith today? What might happen, best- and worst-case scenarios, if you took that step? Share your concerns, fears and hopes with God and ask for His guidance and courage as you take the step.

Jesus Came to Give Us Life

- Both Jesus and Adam were born spiritually alive. Adam died spiritually when he sinned. But Jesus, unlike Adam, *stayed* spiritually alive.

Where do you, like the first Adam, fall short of God's will for you? Confess areas of persistent sin in your life and ask God to help you find strength in Him when Satan attacks and offers temptations to which he knows you are especially susceptible.

Now read Matthew 4:1-11. What does this scene from Jesus' life show you about how to resist sin?

What specific step would you like to take this week to become better acquainted with God's Word so that, like Jesus, you can better resist sin? Start with a realistic goal such as reading a passage of Scripture each day, attending a Bible study or taking your Bible to church so that you can follow the sermon more closely. Let reaching this goal be the first step toward wielding the sword of the Spirit when Satan attacks (see Ephesians 6:17).

What difference does it make to a Christian—to you and me—that Jesus was totally dependent on God and that He did not forfeit His spiritual life by sinning? It's the difference between life and death.

The Whole Gospel

(pages 44-45)

- Many Christians are living under half a gospel. Consequently, we are ending up with forgiven sinners instead of redeemed saints.

What two important points might be missing from most gospel presentations?

Which, if either of these two points, was a surprise to you? Why?

Write out in a simple statement how you would present the whole gospel, including all of the points mentioned in this section.

What a Difference Christ's Difference Makes in Us!

(pages 45-46)

The difference between the first and last Adams spells the difference between life and death for us.

- In 1 Corinthians 15:22, Paul writes, "As in Adam all die, so also in Christ all shall be made alive."

What does the phrase "in Christ" mean to you personally as you live out your life day by day?

- New life in Christ begins when you first trust Jesus as your Lord and Savior, and that new life means a new identity. In turn, that new identity means a new way of living as you live out who you are as a child of God.

How does (or how would) seeing yourself as a much-loved child of God enable you to better live the Christian life?

Satan can do nothing to damage your position and identity in Christ, but if he can deceive you into believing that you are not acceptable to God and that you'll never amount to anything as a Christian, then you will live according to those debilitating thoughts rather than in the freedom and wholeness available to you in Christ.

What thoughts about yourself may be deceptions generated by Satan?

God calls you a saint, and that glorious truth should overshadow the deceptions about yourself that Satan would have you believe.

What truths about your identity in Christ can you use to counter Satan's deceptions about who you are? (If you're not sure, keep working through this lesson!)

Often we have to act as if we love someone before we find ourselves loving that person. That principle of acting first and letting feelings follow may need to function in your life if you are to live out your identity in Christ.

What can you do today to live like a saint, a person loved and called by God, rather than like a sinner, a person hunched over by a sense of unworthiness and failure?

Remember that what you do doesn't determine who you are (for instance, failing at something doesn't make you a failure). Rather, who you are—a child of God—determines what you do if you let yourself believe the truth that God loves you. After all, you can't consistently behave in a way that's inconsistent with the way you perceive yourself.

What Is True of Christ Is True of You

(page 51)

One way to perceive yourself as God does is to reaffirm who you are in Christ.

- In the *Victory over the Darkness* text, you were invited to read aloud the list of answers to the question "Who Am I?" found on pages 51-52. Whether or not you accepted that invitation then, do so now. Slowly read the list of answers aloud. Let yourself *hear* the words and be amazed by God's grace to you.

If you hesitate to read aloud these wonderful words of God's love, what are your reasons?

Which statements of fact are especially meaningful to you right now?

Why do these two or three truths you just listed mean so much to you?

How would believing the truths you listed above make your life different?

You can make the truths you listed more meaningful and productive in your life by simply choosing to believe what God has said about you. That sounds simple enough, but why isn't that step easy for you to take?

Lay before God your answer to the previous question. Ask God to heal those places where you've been hurt, to strengthen you where you've been crippled and to free you where you have been in chains and unable to know His love for you.

One of the greatest ways to help yourself grow into maturity in Christ is to continually remind yourself of who you are in Him. The more you reaffirm who you are in Christ, the more your behavior will begin to reflect your true identity.

The Bright Hope of Being a Child of God

(pages 55-56)

- If you're beginning to think you are someone special as a Christian, you're right! You are special not because of anything you've done but because of God's gracious invitation to be His child. Read again the words of 1 John 3:1-3 and hear the wonder in the apostle's voice.

What hope for today do you find in these verses?

What hope for the future do you find in 1 John 3:1-3?

The hope you, as a believer, have in God is a present hope as well as a future hope. As a child of God, you are being conformed to the image of God and you can begin living according to who you really are—a child of God.

LIVING WHAT YOU LEARN

On 3x5-inch cards, write out the most meaningful answers to the question "Who Am I?" (one per card) and pray through those truths each day this week. Ask God to help you believe these words—words He has spoken *about* you and *to* you—so that you may experience freedom and wholeness in Him.

A WORD OF PRAYER

Father in heaven,

What a privilege to address You as such! I marvel that You name me Your child, and I ask that You would help me believe that I am. Help me to believe who I am in Christ that I may better live out the Christian life as Your witness and as a vessel of Your love and grace. And, Lord God, keep me focused on the race I have to run as Your child. Give me boldness to take a stand for You, unafraid of being different from the people, the culture, the society around me. May I, almighty and all-loving God, depend completely on You, just as Jesus did. In His name I pray. Amen.

LOOKING AHEAD

If you take nothing else away from this lesson, take this truth: You cannot consistently live in a manner that is inconsistent with how you perceive yourself. You must believe you are a child of God in order to live like a child of God.

Chapter 3

See Yourself for Who You Really Are

Every born-again believer is a child of God. Consider how that fact can affect your life now.

See Yourself for Who You Really Are

(pages 57-59)

- Reconsider the stories of Claire and Derek. As a college student, Claire simply believed what she perceived herself to be—a child of God—and so was committed to being transformed into His image and to loving people and growing in Christ.

How did you react to the description of Claire when you first read it in the *Victory over the Darkness* text? What aspect of Claire's journey revealed an important truth to you?

- Derek was well into his 30s before he learned that God is not a perfectionistic, impossible-to-please heavenly Father. He also realized that he already was pleasing God by who he is in Christ.

How did you react to Derek's story? What aspect of Derek's journey revealed an important truth to you?

With whom do you identify more closely: Claire who is confident about her identity in the Lord or Derek who had to learn the truth about his heavenly Father? Comment on the similarity you've noted.

Theology Before Practicality

(pages 59-63)

The experiences of Claire and Derek illustrate the importance of establishing our Christian lives on right beliefs about God and ourselves. We need to understand who we are as a result of who God is and what He has done (i.e., theology) before we can live out our faith (i.e., practical Christianity).

• Many Christians struggle to live out their faith because they try to base their spiritual growth and maturity on practical sections of the Scriptures (what we need to do to live out our faith) and spend too little time internalizing the doctrinal sections (what we need to know about God, ourselves, sin and salvation).

Consider your own Bible-reading patterns. What do you tend to focus on? Why?

In light of what you've read so far in *Victory over the Darkness*, what value would internalizing doctrinal sections of Scripture have for someone struggling with the question "Who am I?"

• When you don't understand the biblical truths pertaining to your position in Christ, you have no ground for success in the practical arena. How can you hope, for instance, to "stand firm against the schemes of the devil" (Ephesians 6:11) if you have not internalized the truth that you are already victoriously "raised . . . up with Him, and seated . . . with Him in the heavenly places, in Christ Jesus" (Ephesians 2:6)? How can you rejoice in hope and persevere in tribulation (see Romans 12:12) without the confidence of knowing that you have been justified by faith and have peace with God through the Lord Jesus Christ (see Romans 5:1)?

When has God's truth served you well in the practical arena? Perhaps the truth that you are already victorious over Satan through Christ (see Ephesians 2:6) has helped you stand strong against his temptations. Also, perhaps knowing that you have been justified by faith through Jesus (see Romans 5:1) has helped you persevere in difficult times. Describe in detail such a time.

In what area(s) of your life are you struggling to live out your faith right now? Outline the situation and then spend some time with your Bible. Find a doctrinal truth that can help you live out your faith in the circumstances you just described.

When your basic belief system about God and yourself is shaky, your day-to-day behavior will be shaky. But, as experiences from your own life may have reminded you, when your belief system is intact and your relationship with God is based on truth, you'll have very little trouble working out the practical aspects of daily Christianity.

- The music director and his wife whose marriage was failing found that, when each of them got right with God, they were able to work out their problems. Getting right with each other began with getting right with God. But what does "getting right with God" mean? Getting right with God always begins with settling once and for all the issue that God is your loving Father and you are His accepted child.

Why would wholehearted acceptance of this truth help two individuals through the problems of their marriage?

What problems would be alleviated by your wholehearted acceptance of the truth that God loves you?

- As long as you believe that God is your loving Father and you are His accepted child, your faith will permeate your daily experience. If you question the finished work of Christ, you will continue to struggle to earn the acceptance that is already yours in Christ.

In what ways have you tried to earn God's acceptance?

What lesson did you learn from the experience?

- Hear these freeing words: We don't serve God to gain His acceptance; we are accepted, so we serve God. We don't follow Him in order to be loved; we are loved, so we follow Him.

What tends to motivate your worship and your service?

Think about your relationship to your spouse, a favorite family member or a special friend. What is it about the relationship that frees you to give and receive?

Thank God for placing people in your life who accept you as you are, thus helping you learn about His gracious and unconditional love.

In order to live the victorious Christian life, you have to believe what is already true about you. Will you have opposition to believing this truth? Of course!

The father of lies (see John 8:44) has deceived the whole world (see Revelation 12:9). If that isn't enough, others will put you down. We have to keep reminding ourselves of these positional truths.

- As you read in the previous chapter, one way to learn to perceive yourself as God does is to reaffirm who you are in Christ. The "Who Am I?" list was designed to help you do just that. Here in chapter 3 you find a supplement to that list.

    In the *Victory over the Darkness* text, you were invited to read aloud the truths listed on pages 64-65. Whether or not you accepted the invitation then, consider doing so now. Read slowly the list of statements that describes your identity in Christ; do this regularly until these truths become a part of you.

Which statements are especially meaningful to you right now?

Why do you think the truths you just listed mean so much?

If you could believe the truths you listed above, how would your life be different?

Ask God to help these truths about the effects of God's grace enter your heart, not just your mind. Also, as before, ask Him to heal those places where you've been hurt, to strengthen you where you've been crippled and to free you where you have been in chains and unable to know His love for you.

Your perception of your identity makes a big difference in how well you live out your faith and deal with the challenges and conflicts of life. And the only basis for an accurate identity is God's unfailing Word.

Relationship Versus Harmony

(pages 66-67)

Perhaps this emphasis on God's complete acceptance of you in Christ has raised the question "What happens to this relationship when I sin?" The grace-filled answer is that your relationship with God is based on the blood of the Lord Jesus Christ. You are a born-again child of God in spiritual union with Him by His grace, which you received through faith. Your relationship with God was settled when you were born into His family.

- Just as you will always be related to your biological father and mother, you will always be related to your spiritual Father. And just as you lived in harmony with your father when you trusted and obeyed him, you will live in harmony with your heavenly Father when you trust and obey Him. (You might consult your church's or pastor's view on this point.)

Consider a time when you failed to take God at His word or when you chose to walk by the flesh—a time of distrust, disobedience or disharmony with God. What did you learn from that experience?

Have you ever worried that you had forfeited your relationship with your heavenly Father? If not, why not? If so, what reassurance did you find that, even in your sin, you hadn't forfeited your status as His child? If you are worried right now, review the truths of John 10:27,28; Romans 8:35-39; and 1 Peter 1:18,19.

Right now are you living in harmony with your heavenly Father or taking advantage of your gracious relationship with your heavenly Father? Explain why you answer as you do.

What can you do to enrich your fellowship with your heavenly Father?

Think about your life right now. What decision or situation, if any, becomes clear in light of this call to obey God?

Know that there is nothing you can do to improve upon your relationship with God other than believing that it is true. You are a child of God, period. The only thing you can do to improve the harmony of your relationship with God is to believe the truth and live in submissive obedience to Him.

Believing the Truth About Others

(pages 68-69)

- As important as it is that you believe in your true identity as a child of God, it is equally important that you perceive other Christians as children of God as well and treat them accordingly.

  The statistics are frightening: for every positive statement a child hears, he or she receives 10 negative statements. What kinds of statements are the children in your life hearing from you? Let your answer prompt a minute or two of prayer.

  What kinds of statements are fellow Christians in your life hearing from you? Again, let your answer prompt a minute or two of prayer.

  Who in your life has been a vessel of God's grace with his or her words of edification and encouragement? Thank God for that person and perhaps thank him or her in a note or with a phone call!

Relating to God

(pages 69-71)

- Many Christians live their lives as though they were walking on glass. They are afraid to make mistakes because if they do, the hammer of God will fall on them. Dear Christian, the hammer has already fallen. It fell on Christ. He died once for all our sin (see Romans 6:10).

How does your behavior show that you might be living in fear of the hammer of God falling on you? Where do you feel—as the missionary did—that you are a failure in your Christian walk?

Do you relate to the missionary who wrote to Neil Anderson? In what ways? How does what he declares in his last paragraph affect you personally?

*   Review the list in chapter 3 (pp. 64-65) that describes your identity in Christ.

What most astounds you about what God says about you and your relationship with Him? How will that change how you relate to your loving God from now on?

Read the truths about yourself listed in chapters 2 and 3 (pp. 51-52, 64-65) often; believe them and walk in them. When you walk by faith, your behavior as a Christian will conform to what you believe.

LIVING WHAT YOU LEARN

What is one thing you can do this week to bring more harmony to your relationship with your heavenly Father? Consider persistent or habitual sins that He can help you resist (see 1 Corinthians 10:13).

Who is one person you can ask God to help you see through His eyes so that you can offer him or her words of grace rather than thoughts of criticism, dislike or anger? Pray and then consider extending an act of grace, trusting that your feelings will follow.

A WORD OF PRAYER

God of grace,

I thank You that my ability to serve You is not what gains Your acceptance, that my ability to follow You is not what determines whether I am loved. Thank You for Your acceptance that frees me to serve You and Your love that frees me to follow You. And I thank You for the security of my relationship with You. May I believe these truths and base my life on them. Help me, Lord, to trust and obey You so that our relationship may be harmonious. And, God, so that there may be greater harmony within Your Body, help me see Your people through Your eyes. And help me control my tongue so that I speak only words that build up, not words that hurt and tear down. I pray in Jesus' name and for His sake. Amen.

LOOKING AHEAD

The Bible teaches that you are a child of God. Nevertheless, you are still less than perfect in your behavior. You are a saint who sins, and that is the great Christian dilemma that the next chapter addresses.

Chapter 4

Something Old, Something New

Being a saint who is alive and free in Christ does not mean being spiritually mature or sinless, but it does provide hope and future growth. Despite God's provision for us in Christ, we are still far less than perfect. We are saints who sin. Our positions in Christ are settled, but our daily performances are often marked by personal failures and disobedience, which disappoint us and disrupt the harmony of our relationships with God.

Something Old, Something New

(pages 73-74)

• In Romans 7, Paul groans, "The good that I wish, I do not do; but I practice the very evil that I do not wish" (v. 19).

What is "the good" that you wish to do but somehow don't or can't manage to do?

What is "the very evil" that you do not wish to do but somehow don't or can't avoid?

If you can answer either of these two questions truthfully, you have personally experienced the struggle that believers have with their old patterns of behavior. A better understanding of this sinful side of your sainthood will help you see your identity in Christ more clearly and enable your further Christian growth.

The Nature of the Problem

(pages 74-76)

Fallen humanity lives "in the flesh," and "those who are in the flesh cannot please God" (Romans 8:8). Since birth we have learned to live our lives independently of God. This learned independence is one of the chief characteristics of the flesh. The flesh is self-reliant rather than God-dependent; it is self-centered rather than Christ-centered.

Until now, what have you understood about the relationship between your old nature, old self and sinful flesh, and your new nature as a child of God?

What have been the consequences—emotional as well as behavioral—of your understanding about the relationship between your old nature and your new nature?

- Positionally, several things changed at salvation. First, God transferred us from the domain of darkness to the kingdom of His beloved Son (see Colossians 1:13). Second, sin's dominion through the flesh has been broken (see Romans 8:9).

How do these truths about your position in Christ affect you? How will you choose to live your life?

Christians are no longer in the flesh, but since the characteristics of the flesh remain in believers, they have a choice. They can walk or live according to the flesh (see Galatians 5:19-21) or they can walk or live according to the Spirit (see Galatians 5:22,23).

We Have Been Grafted In

(pages 76-77)

Concerning your nature, "you were formerly darkness, but now you are light in the Lord" (Ephesians 5:8). Are we both light and darkness? Paul also wrote, "If any man is in Christ, he is a new creature; the old things passed away; behold, new things have come" (2 Corinthians 5:17). Are we partly new creatures and partly old creatures?

Why is it significant that you weren't merely in the dark but were darkness and that you haven't simply moved into the light but are light?

- Neil Anderson used the illustration of grafting navel oranges onto ornamental orange tree stocks to explain what happened when we became new creatures in Christ.

What fruit have you seen in your new life as evidence of having the new nature grafted onto your old root stock?

What encouragement do you receive from this illustration?

In order to grow and bear fruit, Christians must all be organically centered in Christ. This firm rooting is our positional sanctification, and growing and bearing fruit is our progressive sanctification.

A New Heart and a New Spirit

(pages 77-78)

One of the greatest prophecies concerning our salvation is given in Ezekiel 36:26 (*NIV*): "I will give you a new heart and put a new spirit in you; I will remove from you your heart of stone and give you a heart of flesh."

In what ways have you experienced that you have a new heart and a new spirit?

What changes occurred in you the moment you were grafted into the vine?

"You are already clean" (John 15:3), and you will continue to be sanctified as He prunes you so that you may grow and bear fruit.

New Things Have Come

(pages 80-81)

- The New Testament teaches that when you came into spiritual union with God through your new birth, you didn't add a new divine nature to your old sinful nature. Instead, you exchanged natures.

Why is this fact a source of hope and encouragement?

- Your new identity is already determined because the nature of Christ is within you, enabling you to be like Christ, not just act like Him. God knows that you can't solve the problem of your old sinful self by simply improving your behavior (acting like Christ). He knows He must change who you are and give you an entirely new self, which is made possible by the life of Christ in you.

What do these truths teach you about your heavenly Father? Praise Him for His wisdom and love!

Only after God makes you a partaker of Christ's nature are you able to change your behavior. What behavior(s) have you seen change since becoming a Christian?

- You are a spiritual person in Christ. That is your true identity. The issue now is learning to walk in harmony with who you really are.

Since becoming a Christian, when have you chosen to live according to the old way? Give an example or two.

What were the consequences of your choice? Think about feeling or not feeling convicted, and describe any lessons you learned from that experience.

The conviction that comes when we sin is another evidence of the presence of the nature of Christ within us. Sinning is not consistent with who we really are in Christ.

A New Man

(pages 78-80)

What does it mean to be a new man? We still look the same physically, and we still have many of the same thoughts, feelings and experiences. We have to believe that our new identity is in the life of Christ and to commit ourselves to grow accordingly.

If you are a new creation in Christ, have you ever wondered why at times you still think and feel the same way as you did before? That's because everything you learned before is still programmed into your memory. There is no mental Delete button.

• Just as Neil had to learn to react differently to the Navy ship's new skipper after serving two years under a tough old skipper, Christians who have the new life of Jesus Christ implanted within them have some adjusting to do.

Think about your actions, reactions, emotional responses, thought patterns, memories and habits. Name one or two that are still clearly in opposition to God and centered on yourself.

What does the Bible offer as an alternative to the behaviors and/or thoughts you just named? Ask God to help you live according to these models. Plan the first step you'll take, and take it!

As a child of God, you are no longer under the authority of Satan and dominated by sin and death. The old man is dead and new things have come.

New Things Have Come

(pages 80-81)

Despite the fact that at times believers still live according to their old selves, they are new persons—new in relationship to God and new in themselves. We have a new master. Our old master was the god of this world, Satan. Our new master is our heavenly Father. We also have a new nature that is now oriented toward God rather than toward self and sin.

- The conviction that comes when we sin is evidence of the presence of the nature of Christ within us. Sinning is not consistent with who we really are in Christ.

  Describe a time when you have felt this conviction. What happened and what did you do at the time to dispel that conviction?

  When have you found the strength in God that you needed to stand strong against the powerful appeal of sin? Be specific about the details and let this incident help you stand strong the next time you are tempted to sin.

- God has not given us the power to imitate Him. He has made us partakers of His nature so that we can actually *be* like Him.

God knows you cannot solve the problem of your old sinful self by simply improving your behavior. He must change your nature and give you an entirely new self—the life of Christ in you—which is the grace you need to measure up to His standards. What is your reaction to these statements? How might it be expressed in your life from this day on?

Only after God changes who you are and makes you a partaker of His divine nature will you be able to change your behavior.

A New Master

(pages 81-83)

• The death of your old self formally ended your relationship with sin, but it did not end sin's existence. Sin is still present, appealing and powerful.

Stating clearly the points where you are particularly vulnerable to sin's enticements may help you stand strong against temptation. In what areas of your life are you especially likely to act independently of God and commit sin?

By virtue of the crucifixion of the old self, sin's power over you is broken (see Romans 6:7,11). You are no longer under any obligation to serve sin, to obey sin or to respond to sin. Write a one- or two-line prayer based on this truth, and use that prayer to help you stand strong in those areas of vulnerability you just identified.

"There is therefore now no condemnation for those who are in Christ Jesus. For the law of the Spirit of life in Christ Jesus has set you free from the law of sin and of death" (Romans 8:1,2). The law of sin and death is still operative, but you can overcome it by a greater law—the law of life in Christ Jesus!

Saved and Sanctified by Faith

(pages 83-84)

Through God's work of atonement, through Christ's death on the cross for your sins, God changed sinners to saints. This change—this regeneration—occurred at the moment of your salvation. The ongoing change in your daily walk—the process of sanctification—continues throughout your life.

•   Have you, like the pastor who visited Neil, been struggling because your old self hasn't died? Do you, like the pastor, need to be reminded that your old self died at the point of your salvation (see Colossians 3:3)?

    Explain in your own words why you, and this pastor, don't need to be in turmoil over the old self that doesn't seem to have died yet.

    What freedom for Christian joy and spiritual growth do you find in the truths of Colossians 3:3 and Galatians 3:2?

Know that sanctification is only fully effective when the radical, inner transformation by regeneration is realized and appropriated by faith. That's one reason why it is so important to understand your identity in Christ.

- A new Christian is like a lump of coal. With time and pressure, that coal becomes hardened and beautiful. The lump of coal consists of the right substance to become a diamond, and it does so.

  Whom have you seen or known who was at first a lump of coal but after giving his or her life over to God, became a shining example and vessel of His love and grace? (Think about the apostle Paul if no one else comes to mind.) Describe what you saw of the process of that person's sanctification.

Let that real-life example encourage you in your journey toward spiritual maturity, toward being a diamondlike light for your God.

Balancing the Indicative and the Imperative

(pages 84-85)

The *indicative* is what God has already done and what is already true about us, and the *imperative* is what remains to be done as we respond to God by faith and obedience in the power of His Holy Spirit.

Where have you experienced the imbalance between the indicative and the imperative in your Christian life?

What have you learned in this chapter that will help you bring a better balance to your life as you grow in spiritual maturity?

You have to know and believe posititional truth in order to successfully progress in your sanctification, or you are going to try doing for yourself what God has already done for you.

In Summary

(pages 85-88)

Our entire beings were morally corrupt before we came to Christ. Our minds were programmed to live independently of God, and the desires of our flesh are in opposition to the Spirit of God. The old flesh has to be crucified by the believer. There is no instant maturity. It will take us the rest of our [earthly] lives to renew our minds and conform to the image of God.

What circumstances in life helped you recognize Satan's deception and brought you to the point of naming Jesus as your Lord and Savior?

Are you presently living your Christian life as though you were still a slave of sin, much as the freed slaves did after the Civil War? What verse(s) can you claim as your Spiritual Emancipation Proclamation?

The seed that was sown in us by God is only a beginning. Being a child of God and being free in Christ are positional truths and are birthrights of every believer.

LIVING WHAT YOU LEARN

What truth in this chapter was most life changing for you as you began to understand it? How will your walk with Christ be changed as a result of this truth?

What is one area in which you have felt conviction as a result of the truths you have learned? What will you do now to make the changes needed to bring your behavior in line with God's truth?

A WORD OF PRAYER

Gracious God,

Thank You that my old self has died—and help me accept that truth on faith even though I continue to struggle with what my old self taught and conditioned me to think and do. Paul's words could easily be mine: "The good that I wish, I do not do; but I practice the very evil that I do not wish" (Romans 7:19). I'm glad that You understand my struggle. By Your grace I choose to win the battle against sin and stand strong against its appeal. May I find real joy and freedom under my new Skipper. Teach me, Father God, to live so that the

new life within—the life of Jesus Christ—can flourish. I
pray in His precious name. Amen.

LOOKING AHEAD

Sanctification is the process of becoming in your behavior what you
already are in your identity. Spiritual growth and maturity result
when you believe the truth about who you are and then do what you
are supposed to do to renew your mind and walk in the Spirit.

Chapter 5

Becoming the Spiritual Person God Wants You to Be

The story of Ann Sullivan and Helen Keller is a moving account of the power of God's love at work in and through His people. What does it take to be such a vessel of your heavenly Father's grace?

Becoming the Spiritual Person God Wants You to Be

(pages 89-91)

What does it take to be the kind of Christian who can love a person whom others call hopeless? What moves us beyond our selfishness to deeds of loving service to God and others?

- First, Christian love and service require a firm understanding of who you are in Christ.

  In your own words, describe who you are in Christ. Begin with "As a child of God, I am . . ." Then read your words aloud, really hear what you're saying and rejoice!

You can't love like Jesus loved until you accept the reality that, because you are in Christ, you are a partaker of His divine nature.

- Second, you must begin to crucify daily the old sin-trained flesh, to walk in accordance with who you are in Christ and to be transformed by the renewing of your mind (see Romans 12:2). It requires the grace of God, and to live under grace, we need to learn to walk or live by the Spirit. This process is called "walking by the Spirit" (see Galatians 5:16-18), and walking by the Spirit cannot be explained with three steps and a formula.

  Is the fact that it is a process reassuring, frightening or both?

Instead of trying so hard to nail down all the details of the spiritual life, focus on trusting Christ and then let Him move you along in the right direction. You must not limit what life in Christ, the One who died for you, is all about.

Three Persons and the Spirit

(pages 91-99)

Although Scripture doesn't outline a simple formula for living the spiritual life, God's Word does give us some guidelines and important information. We'll begin by considering the distinction Paul made between natural persons, spiritual persons and fleshly persons.

The Natural Person

- This person is spiritually dead, separated from God and therefore living completely independently of Him. Consequently, the natural person sins as a matter of course.

What was your reaction when you studied Figure 5-A (p. 92)? What surprises did you find in the description of how living apart from God can affect your mind, body, emotions and will?

At what points—flesh, body, emotions, will or mind—did you see something of yourself before you named Jesus as your Lord and Savior?

Thank God for the wholeness He has brought to your life.

The Spiritual Person

- At the point of conversion, this person's spirit became united with God's Spirit. As a result, this person lives knowing forgiveness for sin, acceptance in God's family and a positive sense of worth.

The description of the spiritual person in Figure 5-B (p. 94) reflects the ideal. Whom have you known who most closely matches this ideal? What has that person taught you about God? About faith?

At what points—body, emotions, spirit, will or mind—does Figure 5-B (p. 94) suggest where God has been at work transforming you from the natural "before" person to the spiritual "after" person?

Again, thank God for the wholeness He is bringing to your life.

The Fleshly Person
- Instead of being directed by the Spirit, this believer chooses to follow the impulses of the flesh.

Review the description of the fleshly person in Figure 5-C (p. 96). What did you learn about your own tendencies to follow the impulses of the flesh rather than the Spirit?

Which of the following words describe your feelings about yourself and about life: inferiority, insecurity, inadequacy, guilt, worry and doubt?

According to the text (see p. 97), what does your answer to the preceding question tell you about yourself?

•   Believers struggle with the behavior aspect of their growth because they are still struggling with the belief aspect of who they are in Christ.

Consider how you are feeling about yourself and about life (inferior, insecure, inadequate, guilty, worried or doubtful to some degree). Look up the following Scriptures and choose one of the relevant verses to start memorizing this week.

Inferiority—Ephesians 2:6
Insecurity—Hebrews 13:5
Inadequacy—Philippians 4:13
Guilt—Romans 8:1
Worry—Philippians 4:6
Doubt—James 1:5

Most believers live somewhere between the mountaintop of spiritual maturity (Figure 5-B, p. 94) and the depths of fleshly behavior (Figure 5-C, p. 96). Walking in the Spirit is key to the process of transformation, which makes God's people more spiritual.

•   So why are so few Christians enjoying the abundant, productive life we have inherited through Christ? Ignorance, lack of repentance, lack of faith in God and unresolved conflicts keep people from growing. However, the world and the flesh are not the only enemies of our sanctification. We have a living, personal enemy—Satan—who attempts to accuse, tempt and deceive God's children.

What are your thoughts about Satan and his power? Are you ignorant? Are you looking for him behind every bush? Or are you aware of his existence and rely on the armor of God to protect you (see Ephesians 6:10-18)? Explain and support your answer. Be assured that chapter 9 focuses on this topic.

Satan takes an active role in opposing our spiritual growth, but it's a role we can stand strong against when we understand the parameters of the Spirit-filled walk.

Parameters of the Spirit-Filled Walk

(pages 99-106)

No matter how mature you may feel your faith is, you can never be productive for God's kingdom unless you are walking by faith in the power of the Spirit. Again, there is no magic formula or list of foolproof steps for how to do this, but the Bible does help us see what the Spirit-filled walk is and what it is not.

- Know that walking by the Spirit is relationship not regimentation.

What rules or formula for your faith did you begin with or are you beginning with?

What good purpose did or do these rules serve?

How have you moved beyond (or how do you hope to move beyond) these rules to a personal relationship with God?

What the Spirit-Filled Walk Is Not

- Paul clearly teaches that walking in the Spirit is not license. It is not a disregard for rules and regulation constituting an abuse of privilege. It is not doing anything you want to do. Being led by the Spirit means being free to live a responsible, moral life.

When have you learned that what appears to be an act of freedom can lead to bondage?

How have you found true freedom by walking with Christ? Give an example as Neil did to the questioning high school student on pages 100-101.

Walking by the Spirit is also not legalism. When have you been the victim of legalism—whether other-imposed or self-imposed? When have you been legalistic and judgmental in your attitude toward fellow believers?

What have you learned about the relationship between a person's faith and doing the right, Christian thing? Are daily Bible study, faithful prayer and regular church attendance guarantees of a Spirit-filled walk?

Walking by the Spirit is not legalism or license. The Bible's teachings are not to be used as hammers or ignored as irrelevant. Instead, within the confines of God's law, we are free to nurture a spirit-to-Spirit relationship with God, which is the essence of walking in the Spirit.

What the Spirit-Filled Walk Is

• The Spirit-filled walk is neither license nor legalism. It is liberty. As a believer, you are free to choose to walk according to the Spirit or according to the flesh. Walking according to the Spirit does not mean sitting and waiting for God to do it all; nor does it mean running in an exhaustive round of activities, trying to do everything ourselves.

Which extreme—sitting and waiting or running ahead—do you tend to lean toward and why? Talk to God about your hesitation to take a step forward or your tendency to be busy in an attempt to be more spiritual.

What was your reaction to the description of the young ox being yoked to an older, seasoned ox (see pp. 103-104)? In what ways do you try to run ahead of Jesus? Thank God for the privilege of being yoked to His Son in a relationship of rest and in service to the Kingdom.

How are you like Buster, the dog who never learned from his master? How are you choking, or exhausting, yourself by rushing ahead? How have you been yanked forward when you strayed off the path?

Our spiritual walk was never meant to be a burden. The key to a restful relationship yoked with Jesus is to learn from Him and to open yourself to His gentleness and humility (see Matthew 11:28-30). That yoke is also key to serving God. Nothing will ever be accomplished if you and the Lord don't walk together.

Being Led by the Spirit

- When Jesus describes Himself as the Good Shepherd (see John 10:14), He is speaking to our need to be led in our walk of faith.

Do you struggle with the thought that you are a sheep in need of a shepherd? Why or why not?

Consider the comparison between the way Neil drove the sheep ahead and the way the shepherd in Israel led his sheep (p. 105). Why is this difference between being driven and being led significant to you personally?

Thank God that He leads! And He leads hoping that you'll choose to follow. God won't make you walk in the Spirit, and the devil can't make you walk in the flesh, although he'll certainly tempt you to do so.

The Proof Is in the Fruit

- How can you know if you're walking according to the Spirit or according to the flesh? Look at your attitudes and actions, which are the fruit of your choices.

According to Galatians 5:22,23, what is the fruit of the Spirit-filled life?

Do the traits you just listed describe your behavior in the last 24 hours? And what does your answer to this question tell you about your relationship with Jesus right now?

- We must learn to have enough self-awareness to know when we are living according to the flesh and assume responsibility for our own attitudes and actions. We need to walk in the light and learn to confess, to consciously agree with God concerning our sins. When a deed of the flesh becomes evident, mentally acknowledge that to God and ask Him to fill you with His Holy Spirit.

  Is it hard for you to admit your failures and confess your sins? Why? Talk to God about that and ask Him to be at work in you.

Walking according to the Spirit occurs when you choose to follow the Spirit instead of the temptations of the flesh. When you stray from that path, you can admit your missteps and begin anew in the freedom of God's gracious forgiveness.

LIVING WHAT YOU LEARN

Review the ideals reflected in "The Spiritual Person" (Figure 5-B, p. 94). Read again the discussion of the young ox yoked to the older ox, which is based on Matthew 11:28-30 (see pp. 103-104). Now consider your life today. In what situation can you live out one of the traits of a spiritual person? What set of circumstances calls you to walk more in tandem with Jesus than you are currently walking? How will you put into action your answers to these two questions?

A WORD OF PRAYER

Heavenly Father,

I thank You for sending Your Son as my Savior and Shepherd, for that gift of immeasurable love and grace. As I consider all You've given me and my attempts to live a life that honors You, I am aware of how I fall short. Show me where I'm guilty of license and guilty of cheapening Your grace. And show me where I am guilty of legalism toward others in a judgmental attitude or toward myself in demanding perfection. Thank You for Your forgiveness when I stumble and stray. And teach me, Father God, the liberty I may experience in You so I may enjoy a richer relationship with You and greater sensitivity to Your Spirit. I pray in Jesus' name. Amen.

LOOKING AHEAD

As a Christian you are free to choose to walk by the Spirit. Satan does not want you to have that freedom and will try to keep you from enjoying the liberty you have in Christ. The more you walk in step with Jesus, however, the better prepared you will be to recognize and resist Satan's deception.

Chapter 6

The Power of Believing the Truth

Wilma Rudolph was born with major health problems that left her crippled, but after exercising her faith, her courage and her body for years, she became an Olympic medalist and Sullivan Award winner. Can faith do such great things for you?

The Power of Believing the Truth

(pages 107-109)

- Reconsider Wilma Rudolph's account of faith.

What message does Wilma Rudolph's story have for you personally?

Give another example of a person you know of or, better yet, know personally whose faith enabled him or her to rise above incredible odds and achieve things other people haven't.

When has your faith enabled you to stand strong in a difficult situation? Be specific.

What current set of circumstances calls for faith that sometimes seems beyond you? Lift that situation before God in prayer, letting Him know what He already knows—that you're struggling to trust Him.

Faith is indispensable to the Christian life. Believing who God is, what He says and what He does is the key to the kingdom of God.

The Essence of Faith

(pages 109-113)

Faith is the essence of the Christian's day-to-day activity. Faith is the basis for our salvation and the means by which we live.

- First, faith depends on its object. The critical issue is *what* or *whom* you believe in.

What are some of the objects and people that believers and non-believers alike put their faith in during the course of a regular day? Start your list with the example of red lights and other drivers mentioned in the text.

Which of the faith objects you listed are valid and trustworthy?

What does it mean to you that "Jesus Christ is the same yesterday and today, yes and forever" (Hebrews 13:8)?

The fact that Jesus Christ never changes makes Him eminently trustworthy and eternally faithful. Faith that is dependent upon God is faith that can enable you to do great things.

- Second, how much faith you have is dependent on how well you know the object of your faith. When we struggle with our faith in God, it's not because our faith object has failed or is insufficient. It's because we don't have a true knowledge of God and His ways.

Faith in God only fails when we have a faulty understanding of Him. When has your faith wavered because, as you saw later, you had had a faulty understanding of God? Be specific.

If your faith is wavering now with regard to a certain situation, could it be because of a faulty understanding of God? Search the Scriptures. Seek counsel from a trusted and mature Christian. Talk to God about your struggle.

The only way to increase your faith is to increase your knowledge of God. When has learning something about God enabled you to trust Him more?

The only limit to your faith is your knowledge and understanding of God, which grows every time you read your Bible, memorize a Scripture verse, participate in a Bible study or meditate on God's Word.

- Third, faith is an action word. Faith without action isn't faith. If we really believe God and His Word, we will do what He says. What we believe determines what we do. If what we profess to believe doesn't affect our walk or our talk, then we really don't believe.

Reflect on the first time you took a step or made a stand in faith. How did you feel beforehand? What did you learn from the experience? What impact did your active faith have on your relationship with God?

Distortions of Faith

(pages 113-117)

Explain the difference between positive thinking and truth believing. Share your reaction to the distinction. How does the idea of truth believing call you to greater faith?

Read through "Twenty Cans of Success" once again (see pp. 115-116). Which "can" are you going to open right now? Do so by looking up the Scripture reference given and memorizing it.

Believing that you can live a victorious Christian life takes no more effort than believing you cannot. So why not believe that you can walk by faith and in the power of the Holy Spirit? Let the "Twenty Cans of Success" expand your knowledge of Almighty God, the object of your faith, and thereby give your faith the opportunity to grow.

What Happens When I Stumble in My Walk of Faith?

(pages 117-121)

Do you worry that God may be ready to give up on you because you stumble and fall instead of walking confidently in Him? Hear the following two wonderful truths:

God Loves You Just the Way You Are

- The primary truth you need to know about God in order for your faith to remain strong is that His love and acceptance are unconditional.

Who in your life was among the first to give you a taste of God's unconditional love? Thank God for that person.

Do you feel that God loves you when your walk of faith is strong but probably loves you less (if at all) when you're weak and inconsistent? If so, why do you think you have those feelings? And if not, why do you think you are able to rest in God's unconditional love?

Who in your life right now needs a taste of God's unconditional love and acceptance? What will you do to show him or her that kind of love?

Know that, as your loving heavenly Father, God can and does understand your weakness and forgives your sin, and He'll never stop doing so.

God Loves You No Matter What You Do

- Of course God wants His people to do good, but He has made a provision for our failure through His Son, Jesus Christ, so that His love is constant in spite of what we do (see 1 John 2:1,2). Thanks to the powerful advocate you have in Jesus Christ, God will still love you because the love of God is not dependent upon its object. It is dependent on His character.

What have you done that you feel is reason enough for God to stop loving you?

Turn your answer to the preceding question into a prayer of confession and then read aloud this truth: "No matter what I do in life, God is always going to love me. He may not approve of everything I do, but He's always going to love me."

Jesus Christ has cancelled the debt of your sins—past, present and future. No matter what you do or how you fail and despite the lies Satan would have you believe, God will still love you.

Living What You Learn

As Paul teaches in Romans 10:17, "Faith comes from hearing, and hearing by the word of Christ." The only way to increase your faith is to increase your knowledge of God. What will you do to increase your knowledge of God? Set some goals—long-range and short-range—regarding church attendance, reading the Bible, attending a Bible study, meditating on God's Word and memorizing passages from Scripture. Find someone who will encourage you, hold you accountable and, even better, join you in your efforts. Then identify the step you will take this week.

A Word of Prayer

God of love and faithfulness,

I've been reminded of some wonderful truths in this chapter, and I offer my thanksgiving and praise! It's exciting to think that the only limit to my faith is my knowledge and understanding of You, and it's also very convicting. Forgive me for my laziness, for not making time to study the Bible and get to know You better, for not being willing to spend time reading Your Word—for it is Your Word, God, that will teach me more about who You are. Despite all I have yet to learn about You, God, even now I praise You for being eminently trustworthy and eternally faithful and for extending to me

Your unconditional and eternal love and acceptance. What a privilege and joy to be Your loved child! May I share the love You give to me with others so that they, too, may come to know You better. I pray in Jesus' name. Amen.

LOOKING AHEAD

God wants you to accept your identity in Him and live as a child of God should. But even when you forget who you are, He still loves you. He wants you to walk in the Spirit, but even when you stumble and stray, He still loves you. That unconditional, unending love enables you to live out what you believe, to walk in the Spirit, and by your life, to invite others to come along.

Chapter 7

You Can't Live Beyond What You Believe

A basic truth about your spiritual life—and an underlying premise of this book—is that your Christian walk is the direct result of what you believe. And, as the title of this chapter says, you can't live beyond what you believe.

You Can't Live Beyond What You Believe

(pages 123-125)

- The story of Karl's tee shot that opens chapter 7 in the text (see pp. 124-125) illustrates an important aspect of the life of faith: If your faith is off, your walk will be off. If your walk is off, you need to take a good look at what you believe.

When have you experienced "if your faith is off, your walk will be off"? Describe that experience and how your faith got back on track.

- Walking by faith simply means that you function in daily life on the basis of what you believe.

  Think about a typical day. How does what you believe guide what you do as a spouse, friend, parent, homemaker and/or worker? Be as specific as possible.

  Was the preceding question difficult for you to answer? If so, what does that suggest about your faith and your walk of faith?

  What difference does walking by faith make in your life as a believer? Compare, for instance, how you make decisions, choose a profession, deal with newspaper headlines or cope with personal loss to how nonbelievers do those things.

- If you haven't done so already, complete the eight questions that comprise the "Faith Appraisal" form (see pp. 124-125).

  Look at how you completed the eight sentences. What do your answers show you about yourself?

How well does what you think about these eight values line up with what God says? In other words, what do your answers show you about your walk of faith?

If you do not have the same definitions for success, significance, fulfillment, satisfaction, happiness, fun, security and peace that God does, your walk of faith will be faulty.

Feelings Are God's Red Flag of Warning

(pages 125-130)

But how can you know if what you believe is right? You can know because God has designed human beings with a feedback system so that we can know on a moment-by-moment basis if our beliefs are properly aligned with His truth. There are emotional signposts that may alert you when a goal is based on a wrong belief.

Anger Signals a Blocked Goal

- Anger is the first emotional signpost that can alert you that you may be cherishing a faulty goal based on a wrong belief.

  Think about times when you have felt angry and evaluate the preceding statement. Were you angry because one of your goals was blocked? If so, what was that goal?

  Was your goal faulty? If so, what wrong belief (counter to what God teaches) was it based on?

Now evaluate your main two or three goals in life. Are they healthy? Why or why not?

Feelings of anger should prompt us to reexamine what we believe and the goals we have formulated to live out those beliefs.

Anxiety Signals an Uncertain Goal

- When you feel anxious in a task or relationship, your anxiety may be signaling that achieving your goal may be uncertain.

When has your anxiety indeed signaled a goal that you later realized you shouldn't have been pursuing? Be specific about the situation and the lesson you learned.

Depression Signals an Impossible Goal

- When there is no physical cause for it, depression can be a signal that your goal, no matter how spiritual or noble, may never be reached.

When, if ever, have you experienced feelings of depression because you were working toward an impossible goal? Be specific about the goal and how you resolved your depression.

Sometimes depression reveals a faulty concept of God (see King David's words in Psalm 13:1,2). When, if ever, has your depression been linked to a wrong idea about God?

David moved away from his wrong concept of God and its accompanying depression (see Psalm 13:5,6; 43:5). What does David's example teach you? What hope does it give you?

Again, depression often signals that you are desperately clinging to a goal you have little or no chance of achieving, and that's not a healthy goal.

Wrong Responses to Those Who Frustrate Goals

· If your goal can be blocked or is uncertain, how do you respond to someone or something that threatens your success? You may attempt to control or manipulate people or circumstances who stand between you and the achievement of your goals.

When have you attempted to control or manipulate certain circumstances or people who were keeping you from reaching certain goals? Consider the experiences you've already shared in this lesson.

What happened as a result of your attempts to control and/or manipulate?

What lessons did you learn from these experiences?

Why do people try to control others? Because they believe (falsely) that their self-worth is dependent on other people and circumstances. But when they are unable to control, they become bitter, angry, resentful or martyred. The solution for this, and the lesson for you, is to adjust your goals and learn who you are in Christ.

How Can I Turn Bad Goals into Good Goals?

(pages 131-133)

- A faith-stretching question: If God wants something done, can it be done? In other words, if God has a goal for your life, can it be blocked? Is its fulfillment uncertain or impossible?

  Why does it make sense that the goal your Creator God has for your life cannot be blocked?

  No goal God has for your life is impossible or uncertain. Nor can it be blocked. For what area of your life does this fact give you hope?

Just as you wouldn't give your child a task he or she couldn't accomplish, God doesn't assign you goals you can't achieve. His goals for you are possible, certain and achievable. You need to understand what His goal for your life is, and then say, with Mary: "Behold, the bondslave of the Lord; be it done to me according to your word" (Luke 1:38).

Goals Versus Desires

- In order to live a successful life you need to distinguish a godly goal from a godly desire.

A godly goal reflects God's purposes for your life and doesn't depend on people or circumstances beyond your ability or right to control. The only person who can block a godly goal or render it uncertain or impossible is you. What godly goal(s) do you have for your life?

A godly desire depends on the cooperation of other people, the success of events and/or the existence of favorable circumstances that you have no right or ability to control. (You cannot base your success or sense of worth on these desires, no matter how godly they are, because you cannot control their fulfillment.) What is a godly desire or are some godly desires that you have for your life?

You will struggle with anger, anxiety and depression when you elevate a desire to a goal in your mind. When has that happened to you? (Perhaps you didn't recognize the situation as such at the time, but now looking back through this lens you can see what was happening.) What did you learn from the situation(s)?

It's important to be sure that goals are goals, not elevated desires. One reason is that dealing with the disappointment of unmet desires is a lot easier than dealing with the anger, anxiety and depression caused by unreached goals that are based on wrong beliefs.

The Goal Is to Become the Person God Called You to Be

(pages 133-136)

When you align your goals with God's goals and your desires with God's desires, you will rid your life of a lot of anger, anxiety and depression. Such alignment will be easier when you acknowledge that God's basic goal for your life is character development: becoming the person God wants you to be.

- Becoming the person God wants you to be is clearly a godly goal. Nobody and nothing can keep you from being the person God called you to be. But along the way you can be sure to encounter distractions, diversions, disappointments, trials, temptations and traumas that will disrupt the process.

  Life's distractions, diversions, disappointments, trials, temptations and traumas are a means of achieving your supreme goal of Christian maturity (see Romans 5:3-5; James 1:2-4). How have these difficulties in your life helped your faith mature? Give three or four examples.

  What current difficulty can you look at as a means of growing in your faith? What do you think God would have you learn in this situation?

Trials and tribulations can reveal wrong goals, and they can actually be the catalyst for achieving God's goals for our lives—which is our sanctification. When has this proved true in your own life? When have life's hard times revealed to you the wrongness of your goals? Be specific about the circumstances and the goal(s) you were able to adjust after the experience.

Is there an easier way to become God's person than to endure trials and persevere through hard times? Believers who have gone before you will tell you that trials and hard times serve as fertile soil for spiritual growth. God may have already taught you that fact firsthand.

LIVING WHAT YOU LEARN

Review the important distinctions between godly desires and godly goals (see pp. 131-132, especially p. 132). With that fresh in your mind, evaluate your goals. Are they goals or, more accurately, are they desires? If you've never really set goals for yourself, let this be the opportunity to do so. Godly goals and desires help guide our growth in faith. What two or three goals can you establish and align with God's goals for you? Having written down a few goals—be they long-held ones or newly formulated ones in light of the points in this chapter—determine which one you will begin to work toward and what your first step will be, and then take that step!

A WORD OF PRAYER

Almighty and gracious God,

I've read that if my faith is off, my walk will be off and that if my walk is off, I need to take a good look at what I believe. Show me in these quiet moments where my walk is not what You would have it be and where my beliefs are not accurate. I've also read that anger, anxiety and depression can alert me to faulty goals. Again I ask that You would open my eyes and show me which goals I'm pursuing are in line with Yours. May my goals be the goals You would have for me. And, heavenly Father, may my sense of self-worth be based on the value You give me as Your child in Christ. Finally, God, may the overarching goal of my life be to become the person You want me to be. Teach me, guide me, mold me. I pray in Jesus' name. Amen.

LOOKING AHEAD

God's basic goal for your life is character development: becoming the person He wants you to be. And, in the Bible, He offers some basic guidelines for your walk of faith—the walk that will help you reach that goal.

Chapter 8

God's Guidelines
for the Walk of Faith

How do you become the person God wants you to be? By walking the walk of faith. The Bible offers important guidelines for doing just that.

God's Guidelines for the Walk of Faith

(pages 137-138)

- Neil's special breakfast of eggs, sausage and muffins never materialized when his admirable goal was blocked.

When has one of your goals been blocked? Give two or three examples and let them range in importance from your child deciding to be the lead guitarist in a rock band instead of a doctor, to getting to work late because of traffic.

How did you respond emotionally to your foiled plans and blocked goals? What thoughts went through your mind?

Often our sense of worth is tied up with reaching the goals we set for ourselves. When that's the case, life can be a real roller coaster ride. The only way to get off the roller coaster is to walk by faith according to the truth of God's Word.

Proper Guidelines Lead to a Proper Walk

(pages 139-148)

As we've seen, our walk of faith will be off to the same degree that our beliefs about success, significance, fulfillment, satisfaction, happiness, fun, security and peace are off. So let's see what the Bible teaches about these areas of belief. These lessons from God's Word may help you make some vital adjustments to your walk of faith.

Success. Key Concept: Goals

- Success is related to goals. If you're having trouble reaching your goals, it's probably because you're working on the wrong goals.

A good summary of God's goal for you, His child, is found in 2 Peter 1:3-10, and that goal begins with who you are, based on what God has already done for you. God has given you "life and godliness," and now your job is to diligently adopt God's character goals and apply them to your life. On a sheet of paper, list the seven goals mentioned in 2 Peter 1:5-7. Next to each, give an example from your life where you can work toward that goal (for instance, your income tax return may give you the opportunity to work toward moral excellence).

Remember Joshua? His success hinged entirely on his obedience even when God's plan to march around Jericho for seven days sounded quite foolish (see Joshua 6). What lesson does Joshua offer you and to what current situation in your life can you apply that lesson?

Focusing on God's goals—moral excellence, knowledge, self-control, perseverance, godliness, brotherly kindness and Christian love—will lead to ultimate success, success on God's terms.

Significance. Key Concept: Time

- Time is the true test of significance. What is forgotten in time is of little significance. What is remembered for eternity is of great significance.

When has a brother or sister in the Lord done something for you that he or she said was nothing but was in fact instrumental in your walk of faith? Be specific, and then reflect on the definition of significance given above.

What activities are you involved in that will be remembered for eternity? Answer that question knowing that there is no such thing as a lowly child of God!

What we do and say for Christ, no matter how insignificant it seems in this world, will last forever. And that *is* significance.

Fulfillment. Key Concept: Role Preference
- Fulfillment in life comes when you discover uniqueness in Christ and use your gifts and talents to edify others and glorify the Lord.

What does the world promise as the means to fulfillment? Which of these things have you realized, from personal experience, doesn't make good on that promise?

God has a unique place of ministry for each of us, and your greatest fulfillment will come from accepting and occupying, to the best of your ability, God's unique place for you. What can you do today to be God's representative in the following settings?

Your home
Your workplace
Your neighborhood
Your church
Your community
The places you run errands

Find fulfillment in life by deciding to be an ambassador for Christ in the world, in *your* world—and that means at home, in your neighborhood, at work, at school, in your community, wherever you encounter people who don't yet know the Lord and fellow believers whom you can encourage and support.

Satisfaction. Key Concept: Quality

- Satisfaction comes from living righteously and seeking to improve the quality of relationships, projects, products and activities with which you're involved. Satisfaction is a quality issue, not a quantity issue.

When have you experienced the truth that greater satisfaction comes with doing a few things well rather than from doing many things hastily?

Look at your life through the lens of the statement "Satisfaction is a quality issue, not a quantity issue." What does this suggest about how to eliminate some of the dissatisfaction you may currently be feeling?

The key to personal satisfaction is not found in broadening the scope of your activities but in deepening them through a commitment to quality.

Happiness. Key Concept: Wanting What You Have

- The world says that happiness is having what we want. God, in essence, says, "Happy is the person who wants what he or she has" (see Matthew 6:31-33).

It's tempting to believe that things we don't have will bring us happiness. This faulty thinking results in discontentment. Change your focus and spend a few minutes now counting your blessings. List some of the many blessings God has given you.

Was Christ on your list of blessings? Explain in your own words why you already have everything you need to make you happy forever when you have Christ. Read the explanation aloud and allow it to be a prayer of thanksgiving.

If you really want to be happy, learn to be content with life and thankful for what you already have in Christ.

Fun. Key Concept: Uninhibited Spontaneity

- Simply put, fun is uninhibited spontaneity, and the secret to enjoying uninhibited spontaneity as a Christian is to remove unscriptural inhibitors.

What is your idea of fun?

When has (or does) people pleasing (an inhibitor) interfered with your fun? Be specific about the inhibitor: pride, insecurity, the need to be accepted, a desire to protect your image, etc.

Know that you'll find a lot more fun in pleasing the Lord than in trying to please people, so ask God to help you let go of any need to please others, protect a reputation or maintain a certain form of false decorum.

Security. Key Concept: Relating to the Eternal

• The key to experiencing security in your life is to depend on things eternal, not things temporal over which you have no control.

Think about times when you've felt insecure. What temporal things were you depending on?

Read through Romans 8:35-39 and replace some of the general categories listed (troubles, hardships, persecutions, powers or circumstances of the present [see vv. 35,38]) with some specifics from your life. Consider then the rhetorical question: How much more secure can you get than depending on God's promise that none of these things you listed can separate you from the love of Christ?

Our security can only be found in the eternal life of Christ.

Peace. Key Concept: Establishing Internal Order

• The peace of God is internal not external. Peace *with* God is something you already have (see Romans 5:1). The peace *of* God is something you need to appropriate daily in your inner world.

When you named Jesus as your Lord and Savior, you received the gift of peace with God. The peace of God, however, is something you need to appropriate daily. What does "the peace of God" mean to you? Give an example or two of when you have experienced it.

You can control the inner world of your thoughts and emotions by allowing the peace of God to rule in your heart on a daily basis. What do you do to access the peace that God gives?

Know that personal worship, prayer and interaction with God's Word enable you to experience the peace of God, the peace that passes all understanding (see Philippians 4:7).

LIVING WHAT YOU LEARN

As you've read about these eight categories and examined your walk of faith through the lens that they provide, what have you discovered about why you do the things you do? What beliefs do you need to adjust? Which belief will you work on transforming this week?

A Word of Prayer

Heavenly Father,

I know that when You call Your people to do something, You also empower them, and that's what this chapter has done. Thank You for the perspective and encouragement it has given me on my walk of faith and on how You would have me walk. Lord, may Your goals for me be my goals. Help me to develop the moral excellence, knowledge of God, self-control, perseverance, godliness, brotherly kindness and Christian love that You want to characterize Your people.

May I find significance in doing things that touch eternity, fulfillment as I represent You in the situations You have placed me in, satisfaction in doing things for You and doing them well and happiness in my greater awareness of the many blessings You have showered upon me. May I find fun in the gift of life as I stop worrying about my image and other people's thoughts, security in You and You alone and the peace that comes from knowing You.

Help me, Father God, to adjust my beliefs so that my actions will follow and my walk of faith will indeed bring honor and glory to You. I pray in Jesus' name. Amen.

Looking Ahead

Are you ready to change your belief system so that your walk of faith will be on God's track? Winning the battle for your mind will be an important step in that direction.

Chapter 9

Winning the Battle
for Your Mind

Untold numbers of Christians are ignorant of Satan's schemes.
They don't realize that there is a battle going on for their minds.
They are being "destroyed for a lack of knowledge" (Hosea 4:6).

Winning the Battle for Your Mind

(pages 149-153)

What was your reaction—emotional and intellectual—to
Shelley's story? How credible do you find her experience?

You may or may not struggle to accept the very real power of Satan and his demons. If you don't accept the power of the demonic realm, why do you hesitate to believe what is taught in Scripture? If you acknowledge Satan and his efforts to trip up believers, how did you come to understand that truth?

What do you do to battle Satan when you recognize his efforts to deceive and debilitate?

When struggling believers resolve their personal and spiritual conflicts through repentance and faith in God, they too will experience their freedom in Christ.

God's Way Versus Man's Way

(pages 151-153)

Faith in God is the Christian way to live and humanistic philosophical reasoning is man's way, but they are often in conflict. God is a rational God and He does work through our ability to reason. The problem is that our ability to reason is limited and prone to rationalization (see Isaiah 55:9).

- We can live God's way by faith (Plan A), or we can live our way by humanistic reasoning (Plan B).

The strength of Plan A in your life is determined by your personal conviction that God's way is always right and by how committed you are to believing Him. When has your conviction that

God's way is always right wavered? What specific issues have moved you to question God's way?

The strength of Plan B is determined by the amount of time and energy you invest in entertaining thoughts that are contrary to God's Word. Are you, for instance, currently establishing an escape route in case God's plan fails? In other words, are you contemplating your own plans on how to live your life instead of investing time and energy in seeking God's plan and asking Him to help you live it out?

When you vacillate between God's Plan A and your Plan B, your spiritual growth will be stunted, your maturity in Christ will be blocked, and your daily experience as a Christian will be marked by disillusionment, discouragement and defeat.

The moment a Christian wife begins to think that she should get a part-time job in case her marriage doesn't work out, she cannot help but take something away from her wholehearted commitment to Plan A. The more she thinks about Plan B, the better the chances that she's going to need it. Where do such Plan B thoughts come from?

- First, your flesh still generates humanistic thoughts and ideas. You became a new person when you accepted His Son as Lord and Savior, but the old Plan B habits and thought patterns came with you.

On what issues does your flesh speak out most vocally and call you to live independently of God?

- Plan B thoughts come from the flesh, from this fallen world and from the devil and distract you from your walk of faith by establishing negative, worldly patterns of thought in your mind.

  What negative thought patterns, past or present, might have been the result of the influences of the world, the flesh and the devil?

The essence of the battle for your mind is the conflict between Plan A, living by faith in God, and Plan B, living by the flesh as it is influenced by the world, your own flesh and the devil. Although you may feel quite helpless, you need to realize that God has provided all you need to win this battle for your mind.

Strongholds of the Mind

(pages 153-158)

- You need weapons of the Lord to overcome the strongholds of your mind—strongholds that were established either through repetition over time or through traumatic experiences.

  At this point in the chapter, what strongholds in your mind can you identify for yourself?

Consider now the formation sources of the strongholds of the mind.

Environmental Stimulation

- Everything you learned in the formative years of your life was assimilated from the environment in which you were raised. There are two types of experiences that affect you as you mature—prevailing experiences and traumatic experiences.

What were the prevailing experiences of your home, school and neighborhood environments that are still affecting your walk with Christ today in positive ways? In negative ways?

Was there a traumatic experience in your childhood that has developed into a stronghold?

Evaluate the validity and the morality of the environmental stimulation you have experienced and its impact on you.

We all were conformed to this world, and even as Christians we still can be. We might choose to listen to the wrong music, watch the wrong TV programs, have the wrong friends and think the wrong thoughts. We are still going to be tempted to live our lives independently of God since we are living in a fallen world.

Temptation

- Temptation always comes by way of a thought, and the key to resisting temptation is to take that initial thought captive to the obedience of Christ.

God has provided a way for you to escape every temptation, but that opportunity for escape must be seized the moment you are tempted. When have you, like Cathy in the comic strip, let your unchecked, initial thought carry you away like a runaway freight train, leading you to do exactly what you didn't want to do initially? Give a specific example.

When have you been tempted but have taken that thought captive and acted in obedience to Christ? Explain what occurred. (Did God give you strength at the point you needed it? Did you receive freedom once you decided on God's Plan A course of action? Did you walk away from the temptation?)

If we don't capture the initial tempting thought when it first arises, it will probably capture us!

Consideration and Choice

- If you begin to mull over a tempting thought in your mind, your emotions will be affected and the likelihood of yielding to that temptation is increased. Your emotions are a product of your thought life.

"If what we think does not reflect the truth, then what we feel does not reflect reality." Have you experienced a situation similar to the example (p. 156) in the book? What did you fear would happen? What actually happened? Were you able to avoid the temptation to sin in this situation?

Considering the experience you just described (or relating to the example in the book), what could you have chosen to think and do in this situation that could have alleviated the negative emotions?

There are many Christians who don't feel saved, who don't feel that God loves them, because of old thoughts raised up against the knowledge of God. When we tear down those strongholds and take every thought captive in obedience to Christ (see 2 Corinthians 10:5), our emotions will begin to conform to the reality of God's love.

Action, Habit and Stronghold

- When you pause to consider a temptation and then make the Plan B choice, you will find yourself acting on that choice and owning that behavior. And you are responsible for that action because you failed to take the tempting thought captive. If you continue to do that action for six weeks, it becomes a habit or, in this context, a stronghold.

Inferiority, hostility, homosexuality, anorexia and bulimia are examples of strongholds. A stronghold is a mental habit pattern. It is memory traces burned into our minds over time or by the intensity of traumatic experiences. Now, having learned more about strongholds, identify any strongholds that exist in your mind.

- Perhaps it still isn't easy to identify strongholds in your mind. Considering possible sources of strongholds may help.

A woman who was raped while a siren wailed in the background went into a deep depression every time she heard a siren. Has a similar brief and traumatic encounter resulted in a stronghold in your mind? If so, identify that stronghold.

Three brothers learned their various responses to hostile behavior (fighting, appeasing and running away) growing up in a home with an alcoholic father. What strongholds in your mind are the result of the prevailing atmosphere of your life?

Imagine life without these strongholds you've identified. How would life be different for you?

Any negative thoughts and actions you cannot control spring from a stronghold. Somewhere in the past you consciously or unconsciously formed a pattern of thinking and behaving that now controls you. But you need not remain a victim of these mental strongholds for the rest of your life. You can renew your mind.

Renewing the Mind

(pages 158-161)

If the strongholds in your mind are the result of conditioning, know that you can be reconditioned by the renewing of your mind. Through the preaching of God's Word, Bible study and personal discipleship you can stop being conformed to this world and experience the transformation of the renewing of your mind.

- You face more than just prior negative conditioning. You're also up against the devil who is scheming to fill your mind with thoughts that are opposed to God's plan for you.

In 2 Corinthians 10:5, Paul writes "We are taking every thought captive to the obedience of Christ." Thoughts need to be taken captive because they are contrary to God's ways and because they may be the enemy's thoughts. Comment on that fact. What kind of encouragement do you find in this truth? How does it help you as you consider trying to take thoughts captive?

Satan's strategy is to introduce his thoughts and ideas into your mind and to deceive you into believing that they are yours. Comment on the effectiveness of this strategy and identify two or three times when you have realized later that ideas you thought were your own were actually Satan's.

What do these two truths (i.e., taking thoughts captive and Satan's strategy) help you understand about times in the past when you've chosen Plan B?

In light of these truths, what will you do to be better prepared the next time temptation arises?

If you knew Satan had a certain idea planted in your mind, you'd reject that thought, wouldn't you? Disguising his suggestion as your idea is Satan's primary deception. If Satan can get you to believe a lie, you can lose some element of control in your life. If you fail to take every thought captive to the obedience of Christ, you may be allowing Satan to influence your life in a negative direction.

Expose the Lie and You Win the Battle

(pages 161-162)

Satan is a defeated foe; therefore his power is limited, but he still has the power to deceive the whole world (see Revelation 12:9). Satan has no power over you except what you yield to him when you are deceived into believing his lies. What kind of deception are you possibly experiencing due to the enemy? His attacks range from voices in one's mind to mental distractions that negatively affect your personal devotion to God.

Since Satan's primary weapon is the lie, your defense against him is the truth. When you expose Satan's lie with God's truth, his power is broken.

Winning the Battle for Our Minds

· How can you win this battle for your mind?

First, you must be transformed by the renewing of your mind (see Romans 12:2), and that happens when you fill it with God's Word. What are you doing regularly to let "the word of Christ richly dwell within you" (Colossians 3:16)?

Second, you must prepare your mind for action (see 1 Peter 1:13). What imaginings would you do well to dispose of?

In what current situation do you need to actively direct your mind to think about God's truth?

Third, take every thought captive in obedience to Christ (see 2 Corinthians 10:5). What can you do to keep alert and be sure to capture a thought when it first arises?

Fourth, when you are having anxious thoughts, turn to God in prayer. Why is this hard to do when Plan B thoughts are challenging your commitment to Plan A?

When you bring Plan B ideas before the Lord in prayer, you are acknowledging God and exposing your thoughts to His truth. That means victory over your enemy, the deceiver.

Living What You Learn

What have you learned about yourself in this chapter? What plan of action do these lessons about yourself call for? You may need to talk to a pastor or counselor about the strongholds you seem to be battling. It would be a good course of action to get some suggestions about the kind of further Bible study you can be doing as you work to fill your mind with God's truth. Let this lesson you've just completed empower you as you discover in God's truth the effective weapon you need against Satan and his deceptions.

A Word of Prayer

Heavenly Father,

Your words of truth are like a refreshing wind blowing away the chaff and clearing my mind. Thank You for this perspective on your Plan A versus my too often considered Plan B on strongholds in my mind. Thank You that, with Your truth, I can be victorious over Satan's deceptions. God, my thoughts need to be taken captive because Satan often disguises his suggestions as my ideas. Please show me which negative thoughts and behavior patterns are strongholds that Satan uses against me in my walk of faith. Teach me to be vigilant in the analysis of my ideas and diligent in filling my mind with Your truth and turning to You in prayer. God, I want to stand strong in Your truth so that I may experience freedom in You. I pray in Jesus' name. Amen.

Looking Ahead

Again, when you expose Satan's lies with God's truth, Satan's power is broken and the victory is yours. Such victory in the battle for your mind is the undisputed inheritance of everyone who is in Christ.

Chapter 10

You Must Be Real to Be Right

Victory in the battle for your mind is the undisputed inheritance of everyone who is in Christ, and recognizing that there *is* a battle is the first step.

You Must Be Real to Be Right

(pages 167-169)

- Review the story of Judy and then consider these questions.

  How does Judy's story illustrate the chapter title "You Must Be Real to Be Right"? In light of Judy's experience, explain what that title means.

Why are anger and anxiety perfect footholds for Satan?

Where have you not been—or where are you not being—real about your emotions?

Judy's unresolved feelings toward her father and her efforts to cover up her anxieties kept her from spiritual victory, spiritual growth and freedom in Christ. What's keeping you from experiencing these things?

Your Emotions Reveal Your Beliefs

(pages 170-172)

Your emotions play a major role in the process of renewing your mind. If you fail to appropriately acknowledge your emotions, you become spiritually vulnerable.

- As we see in Lamentations 3, the prophet Jeremiah's despair changed when what he thought about God changed. When Jeremiah recalled God's unceasing loving-kindness and great faithfulness, his emotions followed suit.

When have your emotions clearly been the result of wrong thinking about a situation, a person or God Himself?

How did your thinking get straightened out? What change in emotions did you experience as a result?

- You are not shaped as much by your environment as you are by your perception of your environment. Likewise, life's events don't determine who you are; God determines who you are—your interpretation of life's events determines how well you handle the pressures of life.

  What did you learn from the story about the real estate loan (see p. 172)? What did this illustration show you about the connection between events, thoughts and emotions?

- If what you believe does not reflect truth, then what you feel does not reflect reality. Even so, you can't simply change or turn off your emotions. The problem that must be addressed is the wrong perception of the situation that is making you feel the way you do. The solution is to adjust your perception of the situation and base it on truth.

  Describe your general state of emotions right now. If you're feeling more negative than positive, consider whether you are thinking wrongly about a certain event. Ask God to give you insight as you adjust your thinking and know that the emotions will follow.

- The order of Scripture is to know the truth, believe it, live accordingly by faith and let your emotions be a product of your trust in God and your obedience to Him.

Why is it so easy to believe what you feel?

What will you do to know the truth better so that you can trust truth rather than emotions?

"If you know these things, you are blessed if you do them" (John 13:17). In other words, you don't feel your way into good behavior, you behave your way into good feelings.

Don't Ignore the Warning Signs of Your Emotions

(pages 172-179)

Your emotions are to your soul what your physical feelings are to your body. If you didn't feel the gamut of emotions from anger to joy, from sorrow to delight, your soul would be in trouble. Emotions let you know what is going on inside you.

- Think about your general attitude and reaction toward emotions.

Are you comfortable with people's expressions of emotions? Why or why not?

Are you comfortable expressing emotions? Why or why not?

Why is it significant that God designed emotions?

Just as you have learned to respond to the warnings of physical pain and to the red warning lights on you car's dashboard, you need to learn to respond to your emotions. We'll look at three response options.

The Duct Tape of Suppression

- Suppression is a conscious denial of feelings. It is the choice not to deal with them, and it is an unhealthy response to your emotions.

Were you taught to suppress your emotions? Describe how you learned that lesson (through modeling, being reprimanded, environmental influences, etc.).

What have been the unhealthy consequences of suppressing your emotions? How have you suffered because other people suppressed their emotions?

Why are you sometimes or even often tempted to suppress certain emotions? Ask God to help free you from this fear and to teach you a better way to deal with your emotions.

Don't cover over your emotions. Suppression isn't good for you, for others or for your relationship with God.

The Hammer of Indiscriminate Expression

· Another unhealthy way to respond to emotions is to thoughtlessly express everything you feel.

Do you sometimes choose this option? Describe some of the consequences (personal and interpersonal) of indiscriminately expressing your emotions.

Anger is a prime candidate for indiscriminate expression. How do you deal with anger? Talk to God about how you would like to deal with anger and any other emotions you tend to share indiscriminately. Open your heart to His way.

If you wish to be angry and not sin, then be angry the way Christ was: be angry *at* sin. Turn over the tables; don't attack the money changers (see Matthew 21:12,13).

The Openness of Acknowledgment

- If you come to your prayer time feeling angry, depressed or frustrated and then mouth a bunch of pious platitudes as if God doesn't know how you feel, do you think He is pleased? Not unless He's changed His opinion about hypocrisy since the times of the Pharisees!

Acknowledging your feelings is healthy. Not acknowledging them is unhealthy and hypocritical. What keeps you from acknowledging your feelings?

Acknowledging your emotions as a real person is essential for intimate relationship. In fact, it is difficult to maintain mental health unless you have at least one person with whom you can be emotionally honest. With whom can you be emotionally honest? Thank God for that person. If there is no one in your life right now with whom you can be emotionally honest, ask God to give you that important friend and, in the meantime, work on being emotionally honest with God.

So now you understand the importance of emotional honesty and you want to be emotionally honest, but it's unfamiliar territory for you. How do you start? The following guidelines will help.

Emotional Honesty: How to Dish It Out and How to Take It

(pages 179-182)

One of the challenges in the area of emotions is learning how to respond to others when they honestly acknowledge their pain.

• Tired and emotionally depleted, Neil had no words of comfort for the parents whose son had died. Instead, he sat there and cried with them. Later, they told him that his tears had let them know of his love.

   Why do you think we (or, more specifically, you) always feel the need to respond to someone's emotions with words?

   When has someone shown you that he or she understands what you're feeling by crying with you? How did you react to that person's tears?

What people say in the midst of extreme pain is not what we should be listening to. We should be responding to the pain, not the words that express it. In too many cases we ignore the feelings of hurting people and fixate on their words of despair, reacting to what they said or how they said it. Your Savior wept, for instance, when grief-stricken Mary and Martha told Him of Lazarus's death.

• It's important to respond to the feelings of someone in pain. It's also important to not take too seriously the words of someone who is expressing his or her emotions honestly.

Why is this a good rule to follow?

How do you want people to respond to you when you're dealing with some intense emotions and needing to talk them out? (Your answer may be a good guideline for you to follow the next time you're with a person who is hurting.)

You weep with those who weep. You don't offer lectures in response to the rhetorical questions asked out of the depth of their pain.

- Another important point about dealing with emotions is this: Don't forsake love in your eagerness to be honest.

   Remember the husband, the wife, the six o'clock dinner and the seven o'clock meeting? How would you like to respond if you were the husband? If you were the wife?

   What do you do to try to control your tongue so that, when emotions are high, you don't sacrifice love in the name of honesty?

When it comes to acknowledging emotions with your inner circle, honesty is the best policy. But be sure to speak the truth in love (see Ephesians 4:15).

- When you're dealing with emotions, know your limitations. Be aware that times of high emotions are not times for good decision making. Also, be ready to continue a discussion at a later time before you say something you'll regret.

What emotions tend to push you to make decisions that aren't always the best? Are those emotions signals to you to put off decisions until your emotions have subsided?

Is "May we continue this discussion at another time?" part of your vocabulary when you've reached your emotional limits? If so, how has it served you? If not, what can you do to add it to your repertoire?

As human beings, we have limitations, and emotions can push us to those limits. We need to give ourselves permission to acknowledge our limits and stay within the bounds of love and patience when emotions are running high.

- Finally, realize that various physical factors affect your emotional limits.

What physical factors tend to affect your emotional limits?

Which of those factors are you dealing with right now? What are you doing to cope with them?

The important process of renewing your mind includes managing your emotions by managing your thoughts and perceptions. The process also involves acknowledging your feelings honestly and lovingly in your relationships with others.

LIVING WHAT YOU LEARN

Review the guidelines for emotional honesty and choose which guideline you need to work on the most. Then read through the guidelines for emotional honesty with a person who is affected by your ability to be emotionally honest (a spouse, child, parent, close friend, coworker, roommate, etc.). Let that person know what you will be working on and ask him or her to work with you and hold you accountable. That person may also want to choose a guideline on which to work.

A WORD OF PRAYER

Creator God,

You gave me my emotions so that I can know what is going on inside. Thank You for that gift. Too often though, I listen to and believe my emotions rather than the truth. At moments when that happens, please bring me back to Your truth so that I can believe it, live accordingly by faith and let my emotions follow. And, Father God, please free me from emotions I have suppressed and/or my tendency to suppress my emotions. Forgive me for times I have indiscriminately expressed my emotions and show me whom I've hurt and need to ask forgiveness of. Give me the courage and sensitivity I need in order to acknowledge my emotions and to support those I care about when they are sharing their emotions. May I reflect Your love as I learn to follow the guidelines for emotional honesty that I've been reading about. And

Father, enable me to be emotionally honest with You, as You already know what I'm feeling anyway. I pray in Jesus' name. Amen.

LOOKING AHEAD

Responding to your emotions properly is an important step in keeping the devil from gaining a foothold in your life. Sometimes you also need to respond to emotions and emotional wounds left over from the past.

Chapter 11

Healing Emotional Wounds from Your Past

All of us have an emotional history. We've all been hurt along the way, and the emotions from these life experiences can interfere with our spiritual growth.

Healing Emotional Wounds from Your Past

(pages 183-184)

• Reread the story of Cindy and Dan.

What misunderstanding of God's truth was keeping Cindy from leaving behind her identity as a rape victim? (See Romans 8:28.)

Neil explained to Cindy that God works everything for good but that He doesn't make a bad thing good. How might this truth affect Cindy's emotions?

Where can you apply Neil's explanation of Romans 8:28 to your life? And how can this truth affect your emotions?

Cindy needed to be reminded that she is a child of God and encouraged to see herself as His much-loved daughter instead of as a rape victim. You, too, are a child of God. Remember that as you consider hurts from your past.

Bad Things Do Happen to Good People

(pages 184-187)

Any number of traumatic events in your past can leave you holding a lot of emotional baggage. Consider how emotions from the past may be affecting you today.

- As the next two questions will illustrate, those traumatic experiences are buried in your memory and available for instant recall.

How did you react to the story of Cindy's rape? What events from your past determined your reaction?

What names evoke a positive emotional reaction from you? What names bring forth negative emotions? Give a few examples of each and say, if you can, why you react as you do.

The residual effects of past traumas are primary emotions. The intensity of your primary emotions is determined by your previous life history.

- Review the path from "Previous Life History" to "Secondary Emotion" (see pp. 185-186) and then answer these questions.

  When have you experienced the process outlined here? When has a present event triggered a primary emotion? Be specific.

  What did you do to deal with the primary emotion? In other words, what did you do at the Mental Evaluation stage?

  What secondary emotion did you then deal with?

If you handled well the primary and secondary emotions you felt in the experience you just outlined, you may have learned how to resolve conflicts from your past. It's important to learn how to do that so you can deal with the primary and secondary emotions they prompt. Also, resolving previous conflicts keeps emotional baggage from accumulating, weighing you down and even controlling your life.

Learning to Resolve Primary Emotions

(pages 187-188)

Some Christians assert that the past doesn't have any effect on them since they are new creations in Christ, but those who have experienced major traumas and learned to resolve them in Christ know how devastating past experiences can be.

- When you ask God to search your heart, He will expose those dark areas of your past and bring them to light—into His healing light—at the right time.

  Which of the ideas in this chapter are new to you? What are your thoughts about the possibility of memories being buried deep within one's subconscious, the past holding a person in bondage, or primary emotions being rooted in events of long ago?

  Perhaps these ideas are not unfamiliar to you. You may have even seen God, the Wonderful Counselor, work in your life or in the life of someone close to you. If so, comment on God's timing. How did His revelation of the past correspond with your (or the person's) level of maturity?

  Consider praying with David the words of Psalm 139: "Search me, O God, and know my heart; try me and know my anxious thoughts; and see if there be any hurtful way in me, and lead me in the everlasting way" (vv. 23,24). God knows about the hidden hurts within you that you may not be able to see. You can trust Him to be by your side as you feel the emotions from the past and to free you from their effect on your life.

The Holy Spirit "will guide you into all the truth" (John 16:13), and the truth will set you free (see John 8:32).

See Your Past in the Light of Who You Are in Christ

(pages 188-189)

How does God intend for you to resolve those past traumas?

- Understand that you are no longer a product of your past. You are a product of Christ's work on the cross—a new creation. You have the privilege of evaluating your past experience in light of who you are today.

If the hurts happened before you were a believer, you can find hope in the fact that, as a Christian, you are a new creation in Christ. Old things, including the traumas of your past, are passed away. Spend some time now praying about this powerful truth. Ask that God would help you believe in that newness as you deal with emotions and hurts from the past.

If you were a believer when the trauma(s) occurred, what hope do you find in the promise of Romans 8:28 and the perspective that offered Cindy hope at the beginning of this chapter?

· Remember the relationship between emotions and beliefs? Keep in mind that the intensity of the primary emotion was determined by how you perceived the event at the time it happened.

Explain how this truth can help you deal with the primary emotions rooted in your past.

· People who have been verbally abused by their parents struggle to believe that they are loved unconditionally by Father God. Their primary emotions argue that they are unlovable to a parent figure. They find it hard to believe that they are of great value in Christ.

What did you learn from this example of primary emotions, rooted in the past, that contradict today's reality?

If the verbally abused (and maybe you're one of them) began to believe their value in Christ, how would life be different?

Perceiving painful events of the past from the perspective of your new identity in Christ (or of your renewed appreciation of that identity) is what starts the process of healing damaged emotions.

Forgive Those Who Have Hurt You in the Past

(pages 190-197)

The first step in resolving past traumas is to evaluate the past in light of who you are in Christ now. The second step is to forgive those who have offended you. And why should you forgive those who have hurt you in the past?

- First, forgiveness is required by God.

   Read again Matthew 6:14,15. Comment on the inclusiveness of the command and what it reflects about the One who issued the command.

   Like all of God's commands, the command to forgive is given for your benefit. What happens to us when we don't forgive those who have hurt us?

- Second, forgiveness is necessary to avoid entrapment by Satan.

   Why is lack of forgiveness the number one avenue Satan uses to gain entrance to believers' lives? What can the deceiver do with that foothold to block someone's relationship with God?

When have you seen a person entrapped by his or her unwillingness to forgive? Describe the effects on that person.

•   Third, forgiveness is required of all believers who desire to be like Christ (see Ephesians 4:31,32).

Why is forgiveness important in the community of believers?

Why is forgiveness important to the witness of the community of believers?

There are several reasons why we should forgive those who have hurt us in the past, but first . . .

What Is Forgiveness?
Let's begin to answer that question by saying what forgiveness is *not*.

Forgiveness is *not* forgetting. Respond to this truth. Is this a new perspective for you? What does it mean concerning the forgiveness you've extended to people in the past?

Forgiveness does *not* mean tolerating sin. When has extending forgiveness meant explaining that you won't tolerate the same offense in the future? Describe how you dealt with or would like to deal with that situation.

Forgiveness does *not* seek revenge or demand repayment. You can let the ones who hurt you off your hook because you realize that God does not let them off His hook. Why is it hard to leave justice up to God?

- Forgiveness is not forgetting; it's not tolerating sin; it's not seeking revenge. What then is forgiveness? Forgiveness is resolving to live with the consequences of another person's sin. You can choose to live with those consequences in the bondage of bitterness or in the freedom of forgiveness.

Describe a time when you found peace once you forgave someone who wronged you.

Now consider an opportunity you currently have to forgive someone. What's holding you back? Make this situation a topic of prayer.

Expect positive results when you extend forgiveness to those who have hurt you. In time, you will be able to think about the people who offended you without feeling hurt, angry or resentful.

Twelve Steps to Forgiveness

- Forgiveness is what sets us free from the past. What is to be gained in forgiving is freedom. You don't heal in order to forgive; you forgive in order to heal. You don't forgive others for their sake; you do it for your sake. The text outlines the 12-step process for forgiving someone (see pp. 192-195).

Which steps in the process surprise you?

Which steps in the process are especially hard for you?

Comment on the wisdom of the steps and why this process proves effective and freeing.

As difficult as these steps can be, know that forgiveness really sets you free from past hurts.

A Second Touch

- In Mark 8:22-26, Jesus heals a blind man. At Jesus' first touch, the man says, "I see men . . . like trees" (v. 24). When Jesus touches the man a second time, he begins to see people as people.

Why does seeing people as people, not as obstacles, enable us to forgive them when they hurt us?

Where do you need a second touch from the Lord right now? Think about people who have hurt you. Which of those do you need to see more clearly as people?

In a few quiet moments now, ask for a second touch from the Lord that you might see those who hurt you as people who themselves have been hurt. As you do so, know that this second touch is one way God will help you become more the person He wants you to be.

LIVING WHAT YOU LEARN

You've read through the steps of forgiveness. Now it's time to work through them. After you pray the prayer that follows, get out a blank sheet of paper, list the names of people who have offended and hurt you, and describe the specific wrongs you suffered. With that, you will have taken the first step in the journey toward freedom from past hurts. Then move on to the second step, and don't be afraid to invite a trusted friend or a professional counselor to help you and pray for you at this step or any of the others. What is to be gained by forgiveness is freedom.

A WORD OF PRAYER

All-knowing and all-loving God,

I come before You with David's words on my lips, "Search me, O God" (Psalm 139:23). Maybe there is something in my past that, brought to light, into Your healing light, can mean freedom for me. Show me, merciful and gentle God, whom I need to forgive and of what I need to forgive them.

Bad things do happen to good people—to Your

people, God. Help me to trust Your love and Your power of redemption as I look to You to work good from the pain I've experienced.

And, God, as I confront that pain, I hear Your call to forgive those who have hurt me. I know that Your command to forgive is for my own good, but it's so hard. Yet as Jesus hung from the cross, He asked You to forgive those who crucified Him. May I follow His example. Be with me as I work through the steps of forgiveness. May I be aware of Your love and protection as I deal with harsh truth and deep pain. I pray in the precious name of Your Son and my Savior, the One who forgives and enables me to forgive. Amen.

LOOKING AHEAD

Healing emotional wounds from the past will enable you to find victory over the darkness and freedom in God's light. Dealing with any rejection you've experienced is also essential to realizing victory.

Chapter 12

Dealing with Rejection in Your Relationships

Everyone knows what it feels like to be criticized and rejected, and often we know criticism and rejection from the very people we so want to please. All of us have experienced the pain of rejection to some degree.

Dealing with Rejection in Your Relationships

(pages 199-200)

- Most of us haven't suffered the pervasive rejection that Ruby experienced, but each of us has been ignored, overlooked or rejected at times by parents, teachers, coaches and friends.

In chapter 11 you took the first step in the process of forgiveness and listed people who had hurt you. Which of those people inflicted pain, knowingly or unknowingly, by rejecting you?

How has Satan been using your experiences of being rejected to keep you from believing you are a loved child of God? What lies has Satan taught you and ingrained into your mind?

Since we all know rejection, we all need to be aware that Satan uses those experiences to keep us down. But God, who Himself rejected us until we were accepted by Him in Christ at salvation, is able to free us from the pain of rejection and the false messages that Satan has etched into our minds.

When You Are Criticized or Rejected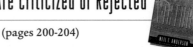

(pages 200-204)

• Rejection, and the accompanying thoughts and feelings, can be a major deterrent to our maturity in Christ.

What thoughts and feelings about yourself do you deal with as a result of the times you've been rejected?

How do you think these thoughts and feelings have blocked your growth—spiritually and otherwise?

There are various ways to respond to rejection, and most of us choose one of the three negative, defensive options rather than the positive approach.

Beat the System
- Some people respond to rejection by learning to compete and scheming to get ahead. Striving to earn acceptance and significance through their performance, these people are characterized by perfectionism, emotional insulation, anxiety and stress. Committed to controlling people and circumstances for their own ends, these beat-the-system people also have a hard time coming under God's authority.

Why is beating the system an appealing option for someone who has been rejected?

Do you know someone who fits the description of a beat-the-system person? Describe the rejection that person experienced and the consequences of this response.

Beat-the-system people are often very insecure. Sadly, their strategy only delays the inevitable rejection.

Give In to the System
- Most people today respond to rejection by simply giving in to the system. They continue to try to satisfy others, but their failures prompt them to believe that they really are unlovable and unacceptable. These people tend to blame God for their situations and find it difficult to trust Him.

Why do many people choose this option in response to the rejection they've experienced?

Do you know someone who fits the above description? Describe the rejection that person experienced and the consequences of this type of response.

People who give in to the system's false judgment can only look forward to more and more rejection. They have bought the lie and therefore find it easy to reject themselves.

Rebel Against the System

- Rebels and dropouts respond to rejection by saying, "I don't need you or your love." Deep inside they still crave acceptance, but they refuse to acknowledge their need. Full of self-hatred and bitterness, rebels see God as just another tyrant and they rebel against Him just like they rebel against everyone else.

What is appealing and even understandable about this response to rejection?

Do you know someone who fits the above description? Describe the rejection that person experienced and the consequences of this response.

This person's rebellious attitude and behavior tend to alienate others, and so the rebel experiences further rejection.

Your Response

Where do you see yourself or traits of yourself in these profiles of negative responses to rejection? Is your approach to beat the system, give in to the system or rebel against the system? Explain, if you can, why you have chosen that option and the consequences of your choice.

Defensiveness Is Defenseless

(pages 204-206)

• There are two reasons why you never need to respond defensively to the world's critical, negative evaluation of you:

First, if you are wrong, you don't *have* a defense. When you're wrong, any defense would be rationalization at best and a lie at worst. Think about times you've been wrong and responded defensively. Was your response a rationalization or a lie?

Why is it so hard to admit when you're wrong instead of being defensive?

Second, if you are right, you don't *need* a defense. The Righteous Judge, who did not revile when He was reviled or make threats when He suffered (see 1 Peter 2:23), will exonerate you. Comment on that fact. How can this truth make a practical difference in your life?

What did you learn from Neil's conversation with Alice (see pp. 205-206)?

As Neil's response to Alice's criticism vividly illustrates, you are not obligated to respond to criticism defensively. After all, the world's system for determining your value as a person is not what determines your value. You are in the world, but you are not of the world. You are in Christ. So if you find yourself responding to rejection defensively, let it remind you to focus your attention on those things that will build up and establish your faith.

When You Are Tempted to Criticize or Reject Others

(pages 206-214)

Rejection is a two-way street: you can receive it and you can give it. We've looked at how to respond when you are criticized and rejected. Let's look now at how to respond to the temptation to criticize and reject others.

- Review the situation of Fred and Sue (see pp. 206-208).

What does it mean to you that you are responsible for your own character?

What does it mean that you are responsible to meet other people's needs in the context of those you live with or any other relationship between believers?

• Relationships don't work when, instead of assuming responsibility for your own character, you attack the other person's character and, instead of looking out for that person's needs, you are selfishly absorbed in meeting your own needs.

Think about the last time you clashed with your spouse, a friend, a coworker or one of your children. Does the description you just read apply to what was going on? Be specific about how you failed to assume responsibility for your own character and attacked the other person and how you were concerned about your own needs rather than the other person's. An apology and request for forgiveness may be in order.

Answer this somewhat rhetorical question: What kind of families and churches would we have if we all assumed responsibility for our own character and sought to meet the needs of those with whom we live and worship?

Instead of devoting ourselves to developing our own character and to meeting each other's needs, we often yield to Satan's prodding to criticize each other's characters and selfishly focus on our needs.

Focus on Responsibilities

- Another way Satan has deceived us in our interpersonal relationships is by tempting us to focus on our rights instead of our responsibilities.

Describe things you feel you have a right to and therefore tend to demand. (The text gives examples on page 208.)

Now consider the flip side of those rights—your responsibility in the given situation, be it your marriage, your family, your job (see pp. 208-209).

What does this discussion about rights versus responsibilities show you about yourself and where you need to be working to become more the person God wants you to be?

What specific step will you take?

When we stand before Christ, He will not ask if we received everything we had coming to us. Instead, He will reward us for how well we fulfilled our responsibilities.

Don't Play the Role of Conscience

- Sometimes we are tempted to play the role of the Holy Spirit or conscience in someone else's life.

How do you respond when someone assumes the role of Holy Spirit or conscience for you? Why do you respond that way?

When have you acted as Holy Spirit or conscience for someone? Be specific about the issue, the person and that person's reaction.

What good came from your self-appointed role as Holy Spirit or conscience? Take note!

The Holy Spirit knows exactly when and how to bring conviction to a person. When we attempt to play the role of the Holy Spirit in others' lives, we misdirect their battles with God to ourselves. In doing so, we often do little more than convey criticism and rejection. Your job is to surround people with acceptance and love. Allow the Holy Spirit to bring conviction and change.

Discipline Yes, Judgment No

- But there are times when Christians are called to confront their fellow believers. When someone has clearly violated the boundaries of Scripture, we are to accept the sinner but not the sin. We are to confront that person in an attempt to restore him or her to fellowship with God and His people, and Scripture outlines how such church discipline should be handled (see Matthew 18:15,16).

When have you seen or been a part of the process of church discipline that Jesus describes in Matthew 18:15,16? Describe the process—how easy or difficult it was—and what happened in the person's life as a result of biblical discipline.

- Be aware that discipline is an issue of confronting behavior you have personally witnessed but that judgment is an issue of character. Disciplining others is a part of our ministry; judging character is God's responsibility.

With your choice of words, you can too easily cross the line from discipline to character assassination. For instance, rather than calling your son a liar (which is a brutal attack on his character), you say, "Son, you just told a lie," a statement that holds him accountable for observed behavior. Think about what you said when you discovered someone doing something wrong recently. Where did you cross the line from discipline to judgment? Give a specific example. Again, an apology and request for forgiveness may be in order.

We must hold people accountable for their sinful behavior, but we are never allowed to denigrate their character.

Express Your Needs Without Judging

- If you have legitimate needs in a relationship that are not being met, you are to express those needs in such a way that you don't impugn the other person's character.

   "You don't love me anymore" has a very different impact from "I don't feel loved anymore." How would you react to each of these statements? Why would you be more receptive to one than the other?

- The nonjudgmental approach of an "I" statement frees the other person to respond to your need instead of defending him- or herself against your attack.

   Do you have trouble asking for your needs to be met? To help you understand the importance of doing so, explain in your own words how *not* expressing your needs can give Satan a foothold in your life.

- When you deny fellow believers the privilege of meeting your legitimate needs, you are acting independently of God and you are leaving yourself vulnerable to getting your needs met by the world, the flesh and the devil.

   How did you react to the poem on pages 213-214? What points support the truths you've been working with in this lesson?

Anybody can find character defects and performance flaws in another Christian. It takes the grace of God to look beyond people's less-than-saintly behavior to recognize that they are saints in God's eyes. May God give us that grace.

LIVING WHAT YOU LEARN

A good first step in applying the many truths of this lesson is to focus on making "I" statements rather than "you" statements when you are expressing your needs. Perhaps there is a recurring situation or two for which you can plan an appropriate "I" statement. Also, talk with your friends and your family about how to express needs without hurting people. Make this a group effort toward eliminating feelings of criticism and rejection in your home.

A WORD OF PRAYER

Lord Jesus,

You know what it feels like to be rejected. You know what I have experienced and how I feel inside. Forgive me for responding so differently from the way You did. Forgive me for trying to beat the system by controlling, manipulating, using and hurting people. Or for giving in to the system and believing Satan's lies. Or for being filled with self-hatred and bitterness, rebelling against the system and against You. Forgive me, too, for finding it hard to trust You to judge those who have rejected me. Help me believe that I don't need to respond to criticism and rejection. Help me to trust You to be my defense.

Then, Lord, there's my criticism of others. Forgive me for such unloving ways. Help me to work on developing my own character rather than attacking someone else's, on meeting another's needs rather than seeking to have my needs met, and on fulfilling my God-given responsibilities in various situations rather than demanding my rights. And help me to control my tongue so that I speak words of discipline, not harsh words of judgment, and offer "I" messages rather than "you" messages when I share my needs.

God, give me the grace to forgive those who have rejected and hurt me and the grace to love and accept those whom I am tempted to criticize and reject. I pray in Jesus' name. Amen.

LOOKING AHEAD

For 12 chapters you've studied growth and what can block it. As this study closes, you'll look at one thing that fosters spiritual growth and maturity like nothing else does—and that's community.

People Grow
Better Together

You've looked at some of the factors in your life that can prevent your spiritual growth. You'll end this call to victory over the darkness by looking at a factor that contributes greatly to your spiritual and personal growth: the community of Christ.

People Grow Better Together

(pages 215-216)

- Danny had gone to the retreat to learn, not to relate. He wanted content, not community. After two weeks, however, he came to see that spiritual growth and maturity happen best in a community of people who know and accept each other.

How did you learn the truth that "people grow better together"? Describe an experience that made that lesson very clear to you.

Maybe you haven't yet experienced the truth that people grow better together. What do you think about that possibility? If you are skeptical, what will you do to find out whether what was true for Danny will be true for you?

Jesus calls His people to share their lives—not just information about Him—with another. That is the secret to successful discipleship and to spiritual growth.

Relationship: The Heartbeat of Growth and Maturity

(pages 216-219)

• In a ministry of discipleship, your curriculum must be the Bible and your program must be relational. Otherwise, you're not doing discipleship. Lots of Bible-based books can be found, but few are the people who will commit themselves to share what Christ is doing in their lives and to help others grow in the grace and knowledge of our Lord Jesus Christ.

When has someone made the commitment to disciple you? Describe the experience you two shared and how you grew spiritually and personally.

When have you made the commitment to disciple another person? Again, describe the experience and how you both grew spiritually and personally.

Discipleship is an intensely personal ministry between two or more persons helping each other experience a growing relationship with God, and Jesus modeled this with His 12 disciples. In discipleship, being is before doing, maturity before ministry and character before career.

•   Earlier questions asked about formal disciple/discipler relationships in your life. Whatever experiences your answers reflected, know that as a Christian you are both a disciple and a discipler, a learner and a teacher in your Christian relationships.

What role do you have in your family, church or Christian community that gives you the specific responsibility of discipling (teaching) others about God?

What opportunities do you have in your family, church or Christian community to be discipled?

As a discipler, you are always a disciple who is learning and growing in Christ. You may not have an official responsibility, but you have the opportunity to help your family members, your friends and other believers grow in Christ through these caring and committed relationships.

Whether you are a professional discipler and/or counselor or simply a growing Christian who is committed to helping others grow in Christ, let these designs for discipleship and concepts for counseling give you some basic practical guidelines for ministry.

Designs for Discipleship

(pages 220-225)

Based on Paul's words in Colossians 2:6-10, the three levels of maturity deal with the issues of being rooted in Christ, being built up in Christ and walking in Christ. Each level is dependent on the previous level(s), and the learning at each level must be experienced in five dimensions: spiritual, rational, emotional, volitional and relational. A point of conflict at each of these five dimensions of application indicates how sin, the world, the flesh and the devil interfere in the discipleship process (see Figures 13-A and 13-B on pp. 218-219). Please remember that there are no clear boundaries between the three levels of maturity or the five dimensions of application as the chart implies.

Level I: Rooted in Christ (Colossians 2:10)

* Being firmly rooted in Christ is based on the fact that "in Him you have been made complete."

Review the conflicts of Level I (see Figure 13-A, p. 218). Which conflicts were especially challenging for you? How did you come to resolve those conflicts for yourself?

If you are a Level I believer now, welcome to God's family! Understand that He wants you to know of His deep love for you and will enable you to work through the conflicts of this stage (and beyond) as you become firmly rooted in Christ. Which conflicts are you experiencing now? What are you doing to work through them? Who is or could be a discipler for you?

If you are mature in your faith and able to be a discipler, review the five points of responsibility listed on page 222. Which one(s) do you need to be better prepared to do? What will you do to become better prepared?

Level II: Built Up in Christ (Colossians 2:7)

- Being "built up in Him" is how Paul described our maturity in Christ.

Review the conflicts of Level II (see Figure 13-A, p. 218). Which conflicts were especially challenging for you? How did you come to resolve those conflicts for yourself?

If you are a Level II believer now, be encouraged during this stage of sanctification. God is at work in you as you grow in the likeness of Christ. Which conflicts are you experiencing now? What are you doing to work through them? Who is or could be a discipler for you?

If you are mature in your faith and able to be a discipler, review the five points of responsibility listed on page 223. Which one(s) do you need to be better prepared to do? What will you do to become better prepared?

Level III: Walking in Christ (Colossians 2:6)

• Walking in Christ means living out our faith in day-to-day life.

Review the conflicts of Level III (see Figure 13-A, p. 218). Which conflicts are especially challenging for you right now? What are you doing to resolve those conflicts?

When you are at this level—and you may be here now—you will find yourself being discipled as well as being a discipler to other Level III believers. With which point(s) of conflict do you need to be better prepared in order to help your fellow believers deal with similar points? What will you do to become better prepared?

The effective Christian walk involves the proper exercise of intellect, talents and spiritual gifts in serving others and being a positive witness in the world. Wherever you are on your spiritual journey, you can celebrate what Christ has already done in your life and look forward to what He will continue to do.

Concepts for Counseling

(pages 225-229)

• Are you willing to commit yourself to being the kind of person someone could confide in? In other words, are you willing to commit yourself to being like Christ?

What are your thoughts and feelings about counseling? Are you wary or skeptical? Are you unsure how to counsel or whether or not God uses counseling? Are you confident that one way God heals is through counseling?

Christian counseling seeks to help people resolve personal and spiritual conflicts through genuine repentance and faith in God. The goal of Christian counseling—whether done by a pastor, a professional counselor or a friend—is to help people experience their freedom in Christ so they can move on to maturity and fruitfulness in their walk with Him. Allow me to give you five practical tips for the formal or informal counseling you may do within your Christian relationships

Help People Identify and Resolve Root Issues
• The first goal in counseling is to help the counselee identify the root cause for an unfruitful Christian walk.

Find Figure 13-C on page 227. When have any of the root causes of a barren life interfered with your Christian walk? What did you do about those blocks?

The fruitfulness of the branches is a result of the fertility of the soil and the health of the root system.

Encourage Emotional Honesty

- Counselees are generally willing to talk about what has happened to them, but they are less willing to admit responsibility and reveal how they feel about the situation. Emotional openness and honesty are key to healing, though.

Why are people so reluctant to talk about their feelings?

Why have you been or are you reluctant to talk about your feelings?

Have you had an experience like the missionary doctor in Africa had (see p. 228), in which you were trying to reach someone for Christ but nothing happened until you were emotionally honest? What occurred?

Unless you model and encourage emotional honesty, the chances of your counselee's resolving his or her inner conflicts and being set free in Christ are slim.

Share the Truth

- Life's hard blows can lead many Christians to wonder what's wrong with them. Their perception of God has been distorted, and they feel that He can't possibly love them.

When have hard times made you wonder whether God loves you? What did you do to come to terms with those feelings and to come face-to-face with the truth that He loves you unconditionally and always?

What would you say to someone doubting God's love in the face of life's pain and disappointments? (See "Who Am I?" pp. 51-52; and "Since I Am in Christ," pp. 64-65.) Speak that truth to yourself if you're still trying to accept God's love for you.

What a privilege to share with hurting believers who they are in Christ and to help them adjust their faulty belief system!

Call for a Response

- Your role is to share the truth in love and pray that the counselee will choose to believe it, but you cannot choose for him or her.

What role has prayer played when you have been a counselee (whether formally or informally)?

What struggles have you had to repent of, first changing your mind and then your ways? Describe one time and let it remind you of what your counselees may be feeling.

Our Lord said to those seeking His touch: "Your faith has made you well." (Mark 5:34); "Let it be done to you as you have believed" (Matthew 8:13). If those you share with will not repent and chose to believe the truth, you can't do much for them.

Help Them Be a Part of the Christian Community

- Help your counselees develop healthy, supportive relationships— family, friends, church. The Christian life was never intended to be lived alone. Progressive sanctification is a process that cannot be accomplished apart from the Christian community.

  How has a strong support system helped you stand strong when life was tough? Describe the support system and list specific kinds of help you received from those involved.

  How have you dealt with the never-fast-enough process of healing and change? What lessons that you learned along the way can you use to counsel and encourage a fellow believer?

The goal of counseling is to help people experience freedom in Christ so that they can move on to maturity and fruitfulness in their walk in Him.

LIVING WHAT YOU LEARN

If you have begun your spiritual journey relatively recently, pray for someone to disciple you. While you wait for that formal one-on-one relationship with a discipler, begin to work through a Bible-based study of spiritual growth on your own. Also, find a Bible study and experience the joy of Christian community as you learn more about your Lord and Savior and His love.

If you are farther along on your journey, ask God to help you be sensitive to His calling to come alongside someone and disciple him or her in a formal way that will mean mutual growth. In preparation for that discipling, work on those points of conflict that you identified earlier where you see yourself as weak.

A WORD OF PRAYER

Gracious and loving God,

Thank You for being a personal God—for sending Your Son who died for *my* sins, who is *my* Savior and who longs to have a personal relationship with *me*. And thank You that I can learn more about You and Your love through relationships with Your people. Thank You for putting in my life people to disciple and counsel me. Use me, Lord, to be a discipler and counselor for my brothers and sisters in Christ. I pray in Jesus' name. Amen.

LOOKING AHEAD

You are what you are by the grace of God. All you have and can hope for (as a discipler and disciple, as a counselor and counselee) is based on who you are in Christ. May your life and your ministry be shaped by your devotion to Him and the conviction that He is the way, the truth and the life (see John 14:6).

RESOURCES

Books

Anderson, Neil T. *The Bondage Breaker*. Rev. ed. Eugene, OR: Harvest House, 2000.

——. *The Bondage Breaker Study Guide*. Rev. ed. Eugene, OR: Harvest House, 2000.

——. *Breaking Through to Spiritual Maturity*. Ventura, CA: Gospel Light, 1992.

——. *Helping Others Find Freedom in Christ*. Ventura, CA: Regal Books, 1995.

——. *Victory over the Darkness*. Rev. ed. Ventura, CA: Regal Books, 2000.

——. *Victory over the Darkness Study Guide*. Rev. ed. Ventura, CA: Regal Books, 2000.

Anderson, Neil T., and Hal Baumchen. *Finding Hope Again*. Ventura, CA: Regal Books, 1999.

Anderson, Neil T., and Tom McGee, Jr. *Helping Others Find Freedom in Christ Training Manual and Study Guide*. Ventura, CA: Gospel Light, 1995.

Anderson, Neil T., and Rich Miller. *Freedom from Fear*. Eugene, OR: Harvest House, 1999.

———. *Walking in Freedom Devotional*. Ventura, CA: Regal Books, 1999.

Anderson, Neil T., and Charles Mylander. *The Christ-Centered Marriage*. Ventura, CA: Regal Books, 1996.

Anderson, Neil T., and Robert Saucy. *The Common Made Holy*. Eugene, OR: Harvest House, 1997.

———. *The Common Made Holy Study Guide*. Eugene, OR: Harvest House, 1997.

Anderson, Neil T., and Elmer L. Towns. *Rivers of Revival*. Ventura, CA: Regal Books, 1997.

Anderson, Neil T., and Pete and Sue Vander Hook. *Spiritual Protection for Your Children*. Ventura, CA: Regal Books, 1996.

Anderson, Neil T., with Joanne Anderson. *Daily in Christ*. Eugene, OR: Harvest House, 1993.

Park, Dave. *Radical Image*. Eugene, OR: Harvest House, 1998.

———. *Higher Ground*. Eugene, OR: Harvest House, 1999.

Warner, Tim. *Spiritual Warfare*. Wheaton, IL: Crossway Books, 1991.

Audio/Visual

Anderson, Neil T. *Victory over the Darkness*. Ventura, CA: Gospel Light, 1999. Videocassette.

———. *The Bondage Breaker*. Ventura, CA: Gospel Light, 1999. Videocassette.

———. *Free in Christ*. Medicine Hat, AB: Hope Resources, 1997. Audiocassette.

———. *Helping Others Find Freedom in Christ Video Training Program*. Ventura, CA: Gospel Light, 1995. Six copies of *The Steps to Freedom in Christ* and two three-hour videocassettes.

———. *The Seduction of Our Children*. La Habra, CA: Freedom in Christ Ministries, 1992. Six audiocassettes or five videocassettes.

———. *Finding Hope Again*. Ventura, CA: Gospel Light, 1999. Interactive video guide on two videocassettes.

Anderson, Neil T., and Rich Miller. *Freedom from Fear*. Eugene, OR: Harvest House, 1999. Two audiocassettes.

Anderson, Neil T., and Charles Mylander. *The Christ-Centered Marriage Video Seminar*. Ventura, CA: Gospel Light, 1997.

Includes *The Christ-Centered Marriage* book, *The Christ-Centered Marriage Study Guide*, two copies of *Steps to Setting Your Marriage Free*, two copies of *The Steps to Freedom in Christ* and two video-cassettes.

——. *Setting Your Church Free*. La Habra, CA: Freedom in Christ Ministries, 1992. Eight audiocassettes or four videocassettes.

——. *Freedom in Christ Discipleship Counseling*. Ventura, CA: Gospel Light, 1999. Four videocassettes.

Anderson, Neil T., and Dave Park. *Busting Free! Video Seminar*. Ventura, CA: Gospel Light, 1997. Two videocassettes.

Anderson, Neil T., and Mike and Julia Quarles. *Freedom from Addiction Video Study*. Ventura, CA: Gospel Light, 1997. Six copies of *The Steps to Freedom in Christ*, *Freedom from Addiction* book and *Freedom from Addiction Workbook*.

To purchase materials, ask questions or schedule a Freedom in Christ conference contact:

>Freedom in Christ Ministries
>
>9051 Executive Park Drive, Suite 503
>
>Knoxville, TN 37923
>
>Customer Service: (866) IN CHRIST (462-4747)
>
>Fax: (865) 342-4001   Phone: (865) 342-4000
>
>Internet: www.ficm.org
>
>Email: info@ficm.org

Gospel Light or Regal books or tapes are also available at 1-800-4-GOSPEL or www.gospellight.com.

Freedom in Christ Resources
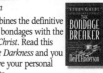

Part One: *Resolving Personal Conflicts*

Victory over the Darkness
by Neil Anderson

Start here! This best-seller combined with *The Bondage Breaker* will show you how to find your freedom in Christ. Realize the power of your identity in Christ!

Paperback $10.95 • 239 pp. B001
Study Guide • Paper $8.95 • 153 pp. G001

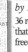

Who I Am in Christ
by Neil Anderson

36 readings and prayers based on scriptural passages that assure us of God's love and our security and freedom in His kingdom.

Paperback $14.95 • 288 pp. B033

Daily in Christ
by Neil and Joanne Anderson

This uplifting 365-day devotional will encourage, motivate and challenge you to live *Daily in Christ*. There's a one-page devotional and brief heartfelt prayer for each day. Celebrate and experience your freedom all year.

Paperback $11.95 • 365 pp. B010

Breaking Through to Spiritual Maturity
by Neil Anderson

This is a dynamic Group Study of *Victory over the Darkness* and *The Bondage Breaker*. Complete with teaching notes for a 13-week (or 26-week) Bible study, with reproducible handouts. Ideal for Sunday School classes, Bible studies and discipleship groups.

Paperback $16.95 • 151 pp. G003

Victory over the Darkness Video & Audio
by Neil Anderson

In this, the first half of his "basic training" seminar, Neil Anderson explores how to resolve personal conflicts through discovering one's identity in Christ, embracing the ministry of reconciliation, experiencing emotional freedom and more.

Videotape Set $69.95 • 8 lessons V031
Audiotape Set $14.95 • 8 lessons A031
Workbook $4 • Paper 20pp. W009

Part Two: *Resolving Spiritual Conflicts*

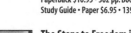

The Bondage Breaker
by Neil Anderson

This best-seller combines the definitive process of breaking bondages with the *Steps to Freedom in Christ*. Read this with *Victory over the Darkness* and you will be able to resolve your personal and spiritual conflicts.

Paperback $10.95 • 302 pp. B002
Study Guide • Paper $6.95 • 139 pp. G002

The Steps to Freedom in Christ
by Neil Anderson

This is a handy version of *The Steps to Freedom in Christ*, the discipleship counseling process from *The Bondage Breaker*. It is ideal for personal use or for helping another person who wants to find his or her freedom.

Booklet $4 • 36 pp. G004

The Steps to Freedom in Christ Video *BY*
by Neil Anderson

In this special video experience, Dr. Neil Anderson personally leads you or a loved one through the bondage-breaking Steps to Freedom in Christ in the privacy of your living room. Includes *The Steps to Freedom in Christ* booklet.

Videotape $19.95 • 70 minutes V010

Spiritual Warfare
by Dr. Timothy Warner

This concise book offers balanced, biblical insights on spiritual warfare, with practical information and ammunition for winning the spiritual battle. Every reader will benefit by learning from the author's extensive experience.

Paperback $10.95 • 160 pp. B007

The Bondage Breaker Video & Audio
by Neil Anderson

In this, the second half of his "basic training" seminar, Neil Anderson explores how to resolve spiritual conflicts through the authority and protection God provides, living free in Christ, training believers to resist temptation and more.

Videotape $69.95 • 360 minutes V032
Audiotape $34.95 • A032
Workbook $4 • Paper 20pp. W010

Freedom in Christ Resources

Helping Others Find Freedom in Christ
by Neil Anderson

This book provides comprehensive, hands-on biblical discipleship counseling training for lay leaders, counselors and pastors, equipping them to help others.

Paperback $14.95 • 297 pp. B015
Training Manual and Study Guide $11.95

Helping Others Find Freedom in Christ Video Training Program

This Video Training Program is a complete training kit for churches and groups who want to establish a freedom ministry using *The Steps to Freedom in Christ*. Includes four 45-minute video lessons.

Video Training Program $39.95 • V015

Freedom from Addiction
by Neil Anderson and Mike and Julia Quarles

A book like no other on true recovery! This unique Christ-centered model has helped thousands break free from alcoholism, drug addiction and other addictive behaviors. The Quarles's amazing story will encourage every reader!

Paperback $16.95 • 356 pp. B019

Freedom from Addiction Video Study
by Neil Anderson and Mike and Julia Quarles

A dynamic resource for recovery group leading pastors and Christian counselors. A step-by-step study that changes lives. Includes video study, paperback and workbook.

Video Study $89.95 • V019

Discipleship Counseling
by Neil Anderson

This series presents advanced counseling insights and practical, biblical answers to help others find their freedom in Christ. It is the full content from Dr. Anderson's advanced seminar of the same name.

Videotape Set $99.95 • 8 lessons V033
Audiotape Set $44.95 • 8 lessons A033
Workbook $5 • Paper 24pp. W011

Setting Your Church Free
by Neil Anderson and Charles Mylander

This powerful book reveals how pastors and church leaders can lead their entire churches to freedom by discovering the key issues of both corporate bondage and corporate freedom. A must-read for every church leader.

Paperback $15.95 • 352 pp. B013

Setting Your Church Free Video Conference
by Neil Anderson and Charles Mylander

This leadership series presents the powerful principles taught in *Setting Your Church Free*. Ideal for church staffs and boards to study and discuss together. The series ends with the steps to setting your church free.

Videotape Set $69.95 • 8 lessons V006
Audiocassette Set $40 • 8 lessons A006
Additional workbooks $6 • paper 42 pp. W006
Corporate Steps $2 • G006

Topical Resources

God's Power at Work in You
by Neil Anderson and Robert Saucy

Anderson and Saucy deal with the dangerous common misconceptions that hinder spiritual growth, including: How can we overcome sin and resist temptation? What is God's role in helping us stay pure? What is our role? What is the key to consistent victory?

Paperback $10.95 B032

Released from Bondage
by Neil Anderson

This book shares true stories of freedom from obsessive thoughts, compulsive behaviors, guilt, satanic ritual abuse, childhood abuse and demonic strongholds, combined with helpful commentary from Dr. Anderson.

Paperback $12.95 • 258 pp. B006

Rivers of Revival
by Neil Anderson and Elmer Towns

Answers what many Christians are asking today: "What will it take to see revival?" Examines the fascinating subject of personal revival and past and current evangelistic streams that could help usher in global revival.

Hardcover $18.95 • 288 pp. B023

Walking in the Light
by Neil Anderson

Everyone wants to know God's will for his life. Dr. Anderson explains the fascinating spiritual dimensions of divine guidance and how to avoid spiritual counterfeits. Includes a personal application guide for each chapter.

Paperback $12.95 • 234 pp. B011

A Way of Escape
by Neil Anderson

Talking about sex is never easy. This vital book provides real answers for sexual struggles, unwanted thoughts, compulsive habits or a painful past. Don't learn to just cope; learn how to resolve your sexual issues in Christ.

Paperback $10.95 • 238 pp. B014

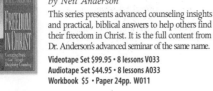

Freedom in Christ Resources

Topical Resources Continued

The Christ-Centered Marriage
by Neil Anderson and Charles Mylander

Husbands and wives, discover and enjoy your freedom in Christ together! Break free from old habit patterns and enjoy greater intimacy, joy and fulfillment.

Paperback $14.95 • 300 pp. B025

The Christ-Centered Marriage Video Seminar
by Neil Anderson and Charles Mylander

Everything you need in one package for setting marriages free in Christ. Thirteen short video discussion/starter segments enhance using the book and study guide. A great resource for pastors, Christian marriage counselors and Sunday School teachers.

Video Seminar $89.95 • V020

Marriage Steps • Paperback $6 • 3 Versions

Parenting Resources

Spiritual Protection for Your Children
by Neil Anderson and Peter and Sue VanderHook

The fascinating true story of an average middle-class American family's spiritual battle on the home front, and the lessons we can all learn about protecting our families from the enemy's attacks. Includes helpful prayers for children of various ages.

Paperback $12.95 • 300 pp. B021

The Seduction of Our Children
by Neil Anderson

This parenting book and series will change the way you view the spiritual development of your children. Helpful insights are offered on many parenting issues such as discipline, communication and spiritual oversight of children. A panel of experts share their advice.

Paperback $9.95 • 245 pp. B004
Videotape Set $59.95 • 6 lessons V004
Audiotape Set $35 • 6 lessons A004
Additional workbooks $4 • 49 pp. W004

Youth Resources

Stomping Out the Darkness
by Neil Anderson and Dave Park

This youth version of *Victory over the Darkness* shows youth how to break free and discover the joy of their identity in Christ. (Part 1 of 2.)

Paperback $9.95 • 210 pp. B101
Study Guide Paperback $8.95 • 137 pp. G101

The Bondage Breaker Youth Edition
by Neil Anderson and Dave Park

This youth best-seller shares the process of breaking bondages and the *Youth Steps to Freedom in Christ*. Read this with *Stomping Out the Darkness*. (Part 2 of 2.)

Paper $8.95 • 248 pp. B102
Study Guide Paper $6.95 • 128 pp. G102

Youth Resources Continued

Busting Free!
by Neil Anderson and Dave Park

This is a dynamic group study of *Stomping Out the Darkness* and *The Bondage Breaker Youth Edition*. It has complete teaching notes for a 13-week (or 26-week) Bible study, with reproducible handouts. Ideal for Sunday School classes, Bible studies and youth discipleship groups of all kinds.

Manual $16.95 • 163 pp. G103

Youth Topics

Leading Teens to Freedom in Christ
by Neil Anderson and Rich Miller

This youth version provides comprehensive, hands-on biblical discipleship counseling training for parents, youth workers and youth pastors, equipping them to help young people.

Paperback $12.95 • 300 pp. B112

Purity Under Pressure
by Neil Anderson and Dave Park

Real answers for real world pressures! Youth will find out the difference between being friends, dating and having a relationship. No hype, no big lectures; just straightforward talk about living free in Christ.

Paperback $8.95 • 200 pp. B104

Youth Devotionals

These four 40-day devotionals help young people understand God's love and their identity in Christ. Teens will learn to establish a positive spiritual habit of getting into God's Word on a daily basis.

Extreme Faith
Paperback $8.95
200 pp. B108

Awesome God
Paperback $8.95
200 pp. B108

Reality Check
Paperback $8.95
200 pp. B107

Ultimate Love
Paperback $8.95
209 pp. B109

Real Life
Paperback $8.95
200 pp. B115

Sold Out for God
Paperback $8.95
200 pp. B116

Righteous Pursuit
Paperback $8.95
200 pp. B114

More Ways to Find Freedom in Christ